GOOD MORNING AND GOOD NIGHT

Margaret de Windt was born on 9 October 1849 in Paris and spent her early years at the Château d'Epinay-sur-Orge, where her parents lived with her great grandmother Baronne de Windt. When she was ten, her family moved to Blunsdon Hall in Wiltshire. Then in 1863 her father was killed in a riding accident, and so when the Rajah of Sarawak, Charles Vyner Brooke, proposed marriage, her interest in the country he held so dear prompted her to accept.

Good Morning and Good Night is the story of this marriage and of Margaret's discovery of and love of Sarawak and its people. Her natural youthful curiosity led her to seek the company of the Malay women as well as the English, and so the reader is treated to the lively and witty observation of this young woman of the people and the culture she found colourful and exciting. This combined with the Rajah's love of his country and his people and his efforts to control the unrest gives a marvellous picture of Sarawak.

The uneasy respect of their marriage survived the death of their first young family. Their second family emerged, and Margaret decided to bring them up in England, and she ages peacefully among her family and friends in and around London.

published in association with Gentry Books

GOOD MORNING AND GOOD NIGHT

The Ranee Margaret of Sarawak

CENTURY PUBLISHING

LONDON

HIPPOCRENE BOOKS INC.

NEW YORK

First published in Great Britain in
1934 by Constable & Co. Ltd

This edition published in 1984 by
Century Publishing Co. Ltd
Portland House,
12–13 Greek Street,
London W1V 5LE

ISBN 0 7126 0348 4

Published in the United States of America by
Hippocrene Books Inc.
171 Madison Avenue
New York, NY 10016

The cover shows View from the
Istana, Sarawak *by Marianne North.*
Reproduced with the permission of the
Controller of Her Majesty's Stationery Office
and the Royal Botanic Gardens, Kew.

Printed in Great Britain by
Richard Clay (The Chaucer Press) Ltd,
Bungay, Suffolk

4035

TO

A GREAT FRIEND OF MINE AND OF SARAWAK

THE RIGHT HONOURABLE

SIR FREDERICK PONSONBY

G.C.B., G.C.V.O.

PREFATORY NOTE

IF readers of *Good Morning and Good Night* detect resemblances to *My Life in Sarawak*, the repetitions are intentional and have the sanction of Messrs. Methuen & Co., Ltd., the publishers of the earlier book, to whom I am greatly indebted for this courtesy.

FOREWORD

BEFORE I start to tell the story of my life, I should like to pay tribute to the memory of my husband, Charles Brooke, G.C.M.G., Rajah of Sarawak, who succeeded his uncle, the first Rajah Brooke, in 1868.

Like his famous predecessor, he strove from first to last for the welfare of the country over which he had been called to rule. The present prosperity of Sarawak, the gradual acceptance of a good government by hitherto uncivilized races, are largely due to him, who, following in his uncle's footsteps, feared neither danger nor hardship of any sort providing he might attain the end he had in view—the betterment and happiness of his subjects. Indeed, were all his actions known and properly estimated, they deserve to be inscribed in letters of gold for all the world to read.

Now all will agree that the first care of a man inheriting some great estate should be that of obtaining a rightful successor, so that he may carry on his work when he himself has left this life. Therefore when the Rajah visited England from Sarawak a year or so after his uncle's death, it was with the object of marrying and founding a family, and, as will be seen hereafter, he met and married me.

He was then in his " forties " and had spent seventeen years in Sarawak, in remote places, living in extreme discomfort and hardship, and leading dangerous expeditions against head-hunting tribes. Sarawak was his whole life, it had claimed him heart and soul. It was not to be expected, therefore, that I, an inexperienced girl of twenty, could interest him greatly or evoke from him any great demonstrations of romantic attachment. But I was hardly prepared for his extremely prosaic attitude towards matrimony and it took me a little time to adjust my ideas to his. Fortunately for me, however, I have always been able to make the best of matters and to enjoy the funny side of things, so that after a while the Rajah's matter-of-fact attitude gradually came to amuse me. When, here and there in my book, I relate incidents which fail to show my husband at his best; and when, from time to time, I deplore his complete absence of a sense of humour, I do so with no disrespect and with no lack of affection. After all, no man is *always* at his best, and no woman who writes her reminiscences can be expected to exclude those in which her husband plays of necessity so prominent a part. I always remember with gratitude his toleration of my youthful inexperience and the fact that he never at any time spoke harshly or crossly to me. I honoured my great man for his efforts for Sarawak, and if at times our home-life seemed to me rather bleak, I soon realized how unreasonable it was to expect great rulers to be " family-men " as well.

CHAPTER I

In the year of our Lord, 1849, on the 9th October, my mother, who had been listening with considerable pleasure to the strains of Rossini's "William Tell" at the Opera House in Paris, found herself taken suddenly ill. She was forced to leave the Opera at once and, escorted by my father, was rushed back to their home in the Rue St. Georges. The doctor (Joseph Oliffe) cursed and swore at being aroused from his sweet slumbers by the urgent summons of my father and—to make a long story short—arrived at the house to find that I had already entered the world.

My parents were a little disappointed. They had not wanted a girl; for my brother (born fifteen months earlier) was such an intense joy to them that they regarded me as something of an anti-climax.

When I was about a month old my parents returned to the Château d'Epinay-sur-Orge, where they lived with my great-grandmother, the Baronne de Windt. The château, which was built in the early sixteenth century, had been the home of the Rastignacs for generations until, during the "Reign of Terror" in France, the Revolutionists overran the country, wreaking their hatred on the aristocrats. They seized the Marquis and Marquise de Rastignac, dragged them from their home and carted them off to Paris, where they were eventually guillotined along with so many of their friends. Happily, their only child, my great-grandmother, had been concealed by the villagers, who loved the Rastignacs, and by some means or other they managed to carry her off in safety to Holland to a Dutch family, friends of the Rastignacs, called de Witt. They adopted the little girl, brought her up as their own child, and one of their four sons, Peter de Witt, fell in love with her and married her. By this time the Revolution in France was over, the country at peace, and Peter de Witt came to France and was able to get Epinay and its dependencies restored to his young wife, the heiress of the Rastignacs. So it was that my great-grandmother, with her husband, settled down in the home of her childhood.

When their only daughter, Elisabeth de Windt (this form of her name had been found more pleasing to the Baronne's tenantry—they thought it sounded less Dutch!), arrived at a marriageable age, my great-grandmother, then a widow, cherished hopes of an alliance with a French aristocrat for her child, but her hopes were disappointed when Elisabeth met and fell in love with Willes Johnson, a gay young spark in the Royal Navy, and the couple were married and went to live in England. Their only child, Lily, my mother, was born in 1826.

In 1842, when Lily Willes Johnson was sixteen, her mother died, and Captain Willes Johnson being unable, on account of his naval career, to look after his motherless daughter, the old Baronne de Windt made a home for her grandchild at Epinay. Again hopes of a French marriage sprang up in the old lady's heart, again to be disappointed; for in 1847 my mother, Lily Willes Johnson, met the handsome and irresistible Clayton Jennings, a captain in the 15th Hussars. The couple fell in love at first sight, and when the news was broken to the Baronne she is said to have shed bitter tears. " Ces Anglais, ces Anglais, toujours ces Anglais ! " she is reported to have moaned when at last her reluctant consent to the marriage was wrung from her.

However, during the first years of their married life my father and mother lived with the old lady at Epinay, which was a very happy arrangement, for the Baronne loved the young couple dearly and decided to name her grand-daughter as her heiress. She made, nevertheless, one stipulation —not a very agreeable one to my father ! She insisted on his taking the name of de Windt, as she said, in a not very complimentary way, that the name of Jennings was much too ugly to be connected with her beautiful Château d'Epinay. Of course he shied at the condition, but Epinay was dear to my mother's heart and finally he agreed.   By this time, at my mother's earnest and repeated desire, my father, though much against his will, had resigned his commission in the Army.

When I was about four years old my great-grandmother died, and my parents reigned supreme over their lands and château at Epinay. Three years later, my brother, Harry de Windt, was born, destined to become one day the great world explorer.[1]   Before Harry's advent my brother George and I were innocent enough to go around our Epinay flower garden peering under leaves and digging up plants trying to find the expected baby-brother.   At last one day to my great delight I unearthed a toad.   " Le voilà ! " I cried triumphantly.   " Il se prépare à devenir un homme ! "   My   triumph,   however,   was speedily changed to dismay when my French nurse rebuked me with the words " C'est indécent, ce que vous faîtes là ! "   Instead of the gratitude I had expected for my discovery I found myself severely snubbed.   I couldn't understand it at all.

However much I love Frenchwomen I do not consider they make as good children's nurses as Englishwomen do.   The French are affectionate and kind, and yet in my day our nurses thought nothing of frightening us children into good behaviour.   When we were loath to return indoors from our play in the garden, Marie and

[1] Harry de Windt died in November 1933, loved by all who knew him.

Virginie would put sheets over their heads and scream at us from our nursery windows, " Les revenants vont vous attraper ! Ils viennent vous chercher du cimetière ! " Also, they could never resist making capital out of a thunderstorm, exclaiming at an unusually loud peal of thunder, " Ecoutez ! Dieu est très fâché avec vous ! " to which I retorted one day, " Le Bon Dieu, comme il se donne du mal pour moi ! " This piece of repartee deprived me of my portion of cake for tea.

But in spite of our nurses and their queer ways our early years spent at Epinay were happy. My parents were apt to become rather bored with my brother and myself by noon, but took a good deal of trouble with us in the morning, somewhat to the astonishment of our neighbours, the Vigiers, whose château was situated only a few miles from our own. Before her marriage Baroness Vigier had been the noted *cantatrice* Cruvelli. She nearly fainted one day on beholding me—aged four—cantering down her drive on a Shetland pony, my father following on foot, armed with a large whip, urging us along. It was he who taught me to ride almost from babyhood. The Vigier lady shook her fist at him, crying in horror, " Mais vous allez la tuer, cette petite ! " whilst I, scarlet in the face and giggling with mirth, belied her well-meant warning.

Music was one of my father's delights. At the same tender age (four) my fingers were laid on

the piano. At five I could read music and play
tunes ; and at seven I was launched into concerted
music and strummed away at the easier Trios of
Mozart, unknown and somewhat poverty-stricken
artists (violins and 'cellos) from modest orchestras
in Paris being bidden to Epinay to play concerted
music with my brother and myself.

Yes, I loved Epinay, the village people and,
above all, le père Julien, the Curé. I was sent
to his presbytère every Sunday at midday, after
Mass, when he would tell me about the Bon
Dieu, teach me the Lord's Prayer in French and,
if I had been *very* good, invite me to share his
déjeuner.

These were always Special Occasions for me !
After crossing ourselves and he had said grace in
Latin (of which I did not understand one word)
we would partake of œufs à la coque, into which
we would dip what he called " douillettes " (thin
pieces of bread-and-butter). This I thought an
altogether delicious treat, not being allowed to
indulge in similar practices at home. The Curé's
meal would come to an end with oranges or
apples or sometimes chasselas, the good man
priding himself on the grapes having come from
the famous chasselas at Fontainebleau, although
some of his friends used to appear slightly incredulous about this. I remember, too, the café
noir which concluded the repast, and the way he
would dip a large spoon filled with pieces of white
sugar into the dark liquid, afterwards transferring

it into my open and expectant mouth. " Des canards, ma petite ; c'est bon—n'est-ce-pas ? " I heartily agreed, and loved the Curé dearly. " Maintenant, à genoux, mon enfant—ma bénédiction ! " Then I would kneel, and as he made the sign of the Cross over me would feel that the Bon Dieu and his Angels were descending on me at his bidding. . . .

How blessed it is, when one has grown aged and bruised with the hurtlings of the world, to recapture for a few moments the peace and beauty of those childhood days ! Thank goodness, their memory remains to soothe and help one in these difficult times of Unbelief, when it would sometimes seem as though the worship of Machinery had ousted the worship of High and Holy things from the hearts and minds of all sorts and conditions of men.

At Epinay, too, we children were filled with delight when allowed to mingle with the villagers, who, when garnering their apples from the orchards around, would perch us children high on the top of the rosy-fruit-laden carts as they were driven slowly home to the village. They gave me the name of " la petite Baronne," for they said I so much resembled my great-grandmother. This made me feel very happy, for I knew how well they had loved her. A personage of great interest to me was Monsieur Lacombe—a man of about sixty-five years of age—Maire of Epinay at that time, for, when a seven-year-old boy in Paris, he had seen Queen Marie Antoinette drawn in a cart to her execution. . . .

After all, the country of one's birth, which one has lived in and loved in childhood's days, must always be the closest to one's heart—nearer than any other. France has always remained for me my most beloved land. No rose smells as sweet to me as those that grew in my garden at Epinay, and even to this day I feel more at home with a party of French friends than with a party of my own countrymen. Not that I do not realize that England is the greatest country in the world and that English men and women are in their character, their loyalty, their truth, above all others. But to me the French are so lovable in this sense, that if they take to you they will talk to you from their hearts. They are so entirely free from that English reserve which almost amounts to a bugbear—the fear of *giving themselves away*. Such a thought would never cross the mind of the darling French. If, on meeting one for the first time, they feel that " surtout il a du cœur," it is a mark of approval so high that it might almost be a talisman admitting one straightway into their affection. I cannot imagine (but this may be my mistake) that the English care—or even wonder —whether a new acquaintance has a sympathetic heart or no.

I always look upon my first ten years—the Epinay years—as the happiest of my life. When our birthdays came round, the village people,

under the direction of the Maire, Monsieur Lacombe, would come in procession to our house,
bringing us bouquets from their gardens, and a
beautiful wreath of violets, primroses, roses or
chrysanthemums with which we would be
crowned with all ceremony. My birthday falling
in October, mine was always a chrysanthemum
wreath, and well do I remember how the long
lovely petals would fall over my eyes and tickle
my nose.

.   .   .   .   .

But alas! As time went on, confidence in the
stability of Napoleon III's government and the
safety of property in France began to wane.
The French people were becoming restless again.
The Emperor, attacked by the malady that later
ended his life at Chislehurst, had lost the prestige
that had helped to restore prosperity and con-
tentment to France for the past few years. My
father's and mother's trustees were English and
they viewed with misgiving the political outlook
in France. Moreover, my brothers, having been
born and brought up in France, would naturally
be called to the French Army when they reached
military age. Furthermore, my father had, at
his uncle's death, become possessor of valuable
coal-mines in Northumberland. All these con-
siderations carried great weight with the trustees
as well as with my mother's father, and ended in
their insisting on my mother selling her beloved
Epinay and its many acres and, out of the

proceeds of the sale, my parents buying for themselves a property in England where their children would be brought up as English subjects.

Eventually Epinay was sold, the purchaser being a Spanish grandee who gave full value for the estate.

My father now bought a property in Wiltshire, at a place called Blunsdon, about seven miles from Hannington Hall, where my mother's father, Captain Willes Johnson, had made his home. My mother was heart-broken at leaving Epinay ; but my father, I imagine, was rather pleased. As for me, I wept bitter tears when I bade good-bye to my beloved Curé and to the village people who had been my dear friends.

My parents then began to build themselves a large house on the Wiltshire estate. In order to furnish ampler sums for the erection of a somewhat grand and imposing structure, they decided to effect certain economies by retiring to Boulogne-sur-Mer until such time as their new home should be ready to receive them. How I hated the ugly house which sheltered us at Boulogne !—chosen, I suppose, because it was large enough for our numerous household. For we were numerous—my parents, my brothers and myself, my father's butler, his valet, my mother's maid—a cook, housemaids, kitchenmaids and so on. My elder brother was sent to a college in the town, but only as a day scholar, my younger brother was left in the care of a French nurse, whilst I was provided with an odious French governess who used to beat me and lock me up in dark airless cupboards when she said I had been naughty, I never daring to complain or tell tales. The house looked on to a dirty street in front and on to a courtyard at the back ; my schoolroom, bare of windows, was lighted only by a glass partition from the corridor and a window high up near the ceiling, which opened and shut by cords and pulleys from below. No one, I think, ever realized how I ate my childish heart out, transplanted to this hideous place from my paradise at Epinay. We stayed in Boulogne for three years. I seldom had any children to play with, my governess treated me abominably and we saw very little of our parents. Occasionally they would send for us after dinner and we would sit beside them at dessert. My father gave my elder brother and myself music lessons in the morning, but there our drawing nigh to our parents ended. So passed these three years, at the end of which my French governess, who was found to be insane, was sent away and eventually placed in a lunatic asylum in Paris.

CHAPTER II

At last Blunsdon Hall, our house in Wiltshire, was completed and, bag and baggage, we all set out for England.

Even as a child I always looked upon our new home as the ugliest place I had ever seen. It was a mansion set upon a hill, built in the " faux gothique " style, a type of residence frequently built at that period, examples of which are still, unfortunately, to be seen. It was ornamental to the last degree, with all its pretentious nonsense —gables terminated by bronze dragons, tiny pennants on which were emblazoned portions of the owner's coat-of-arms; the structure being completed by a castellated tower over which a flag was flown when the owner was in residence. It was beyond my comprehension how my father and mother could ever have managed to rear up such a place. Its one redeeming feature was its roominess. It contained some forty bedrooms, bathrooms galore, a vast hall panelled in oak, a boudoir, a good-sized library and an immense dining-room and drawing-room *en suite*.

My grandfather, Captain Willes Johnson, and Mrs. Willes Johnson—a Welsh lady whom he had married *en seconde noce*, were very popular and much loved in the county, but in spite of our being their close relatives I imagine that my father and mother found some difficulty in gaining the recognition that was their due. After all, from the fox-hunting squires' point of view, we really were neither fish, flesh, fowl nor good red herring. Here we were, building ourselves a new house and establishing ourselves in a county whose magnates think nothing of folk whose family tree is not deeply rooted in the neighbourhood of Battle Abbey. "Who has ever heard of the de Windts in Wiltshire?" I can fancy them saying when my parents presumed to take up residence in their immaculate county. What a difference nowadays, however, when times have changed, and Mr. Hiram Z. Bloggs, U.S.A., however badly bred, would be sure of a friendly welcome in any English county provided he were wealthy enough to buy his way into its society.

My father, it is true, had been an officer in the 15th Hussars and had been of good service to his country; but he belonged to Northumberland, and Wiltshire had nothing to do with that county. Moreover, having lived at Epinay for so many years with my mother, he had caught many of the French ways and fashions. Napoleon III waxed his moustachios, Frenchmen did the same; my father followed the fashion and waxed his. Although he was a tall and very handsome man with dark hair, blue eyes and well-shaped brows, he must, with his waxed moustachios, have appeared rather quaint to the mutton-chop-be-whiskered, hunting, sporting men in Wiltshire. They were said to have found a remarkable resemblance between my father and the French Emperor, in spite of the fact that the latter was short, squat and rather ugly. But the waxed moustachios had done the mischief! When one considers too that we all—including my mother —found it much easier to express ourselves in French than in English, one can hardly wonder if (to mix one's metaphor) we appeared to the English County like so many mushrooms sprung up over-night on the top of Blunsdon Hill. However, the County people came to call and my mother, in spite of her dislike to Blunsdon and everything connected with it (for she could never forget Epinay), duly returned the calls; but it was all much against the grain. She made few real friends in the neighbourhood and much preferred the society of several adoring spinsters of uncertain age whom she had known for years before we came to Wiltshire.

My brothers were sent to English schools, my father bought four or five hunters, and I was given a pony on which I was sometimes allowed to ride to the meets near by. My parents did not pay a great deal of attention to me—on account of my being a girl, I suppose—but I was provided with a German governess who hailed from Hanover. Fräulein would set me German verbs to learn by heart—" Ich bin—du bist " and so on

—and then, sinking into the one comfortable arm-chair in the school-room, would proceed to knit an endless number of woollen socks for a German gentleman—a shopkeeper in London—to whom she was engaged. Our afternoons were mostly spent in surreptitiously cutting flowers from the garden to send to her fiancé at his London lodgings. In summer our walks were almost always directed to certain pools situated in our fields where forget-me-nots were in bloom. Handfuls of the lovely flowers would be torn from their watery homes and placed in pudding basins, from which prosaic moulds they would emerge as wreaths, when sentimental Fräulein, alive to the necessity of giving me *some* instruction in German, would make me write on perforated cards in German characters the words " Oh du mein holde Abend stern, Vergiss mein nicht ! "

At the end of a year Fräulein left us, to be married to her swain. An English lady, young and very charming, took her place. This lady was a good musician and an exceptionally good pianist. She encouraged my playing. I began to learn Beethoven and Mozart by heart under her tuition. She was well educated and very well read. Between lessons she would read *Waverley* to me, which made me cry ; and *Pickwick*, which made me laugh. She would also read me daily one of the Psalms. " Hear the music of these words," the dear thing used to say. " Young as you are, you ought to be able to feel your way through the more beautiful to the more ordinary prose." Once or twice she attempted Shakespeare, but—to my shame be it said—his immortal words then fell on deaf ears. Perhaps at that time I was not yet English enough to appreciate the divine Bard.

A year or two went by, comparatively happy ones for me. Although I had no other children to play with I had my governess, and she was my constant companion.

One oppressively hot day—the 3rd of August, 1863—my father mounted his favourite hunter at our hall door, on his way to call on my grandfather's widow (my grandfather having died the week before). My father had bought the mare when he first came to Blunsdon. She was good-tempered and well-mannered and he had named her " Betsy Baker " after an English farce in an amateur performance of which he and my mother had taken part. On his way to Hannington Hall the animal bolted and collided with a turnpike that barred the road. The impact was so violent that it sent horse and rider hurtling into a deep ditch; the mare, turning a somersault, landed on her back, killing my father, who lay crushed beneath her. . . .

The news was broken as tenderly as possible to my mother, who was prostrated with grief. We children, too, cried our hearts out, for we had really loved our father, and now that he had been so suddenly torn from us the memory of his many kindnesses completely overwhelmed us.

From that time on, our lives were entirely changed. My mother's dislike of Blunsdon became intensified into hatred by my father's death. My dear governess left us. Our home was broken up, and we never again settled down for any length of time.

My mother engaged an English tutor for my elder brother and a French governess for me—a Roman Catholic lady of some fifty years, and as bigoted as she could be. One or two of the spinster lady friends, to whom I have already alluded, constituted themselves my mother's inseparable companions and never left her side. They interfered with all we did and gave us not one moment's peace, so that it is not surprising that we children disliked them intensely. My mother seemed incapable of remaining in one place for more than a few weeks, so that we were perpetually journeying here, there and everywhere, accompanied by quite a large entourage over which the parasitical spinsters held sway. From Paris to Florence—from Florence to Rome —Switzerland—the Tyrol, on we would move, always living in hotels, knowing no one of any consequence, for my mother was bored with so-called society and much preferred the company of her spinsters. All these wanderings must have cost my mother large sums, but she was sole mistress of her fortune and pursued her way according to her fancy.

During the first few years of our nomadic existence my mother revisited Blunsdon for two or three weeks at a time, but those visits only resulted in her detesting the place the more, and finally she decided to sell it. (Incidentally, the people who purchased the ornate and castellated residence found it exactly to their taste and became quite popular with the County.)

My mother now found it desirable to acquire a *pied-à-terre* in which to house her furniture, pictures, plate and other belongings, and rented a property near Highworth, in Wiltshire, called Warneford Place, belonging to a family of that name.

By this time I was eighteen and quite grown up, my governesses were discarded, and I had to get on with my life as best I could. My great-uncles and great-aunts, some five or six in number, now began to bestir themselves on my behalf. "What are you doing about Margaret?" they asked my mother. "You must bring her to London for the season. She ought to be presented and meet eligible *partis*." But my mother turned a deaf ear, would listen to nothing about London, my presentation at Court or eligible *partis*.

At this juncture, however, Lady Vane (Lady Edwardes' daughter, and first cousin to my mother) came to visit us at Warneford, took a fancy to me, and persuaded my mother to let her present me at one of Queen Victoria's Drawing-Rooms. Everyone who knew Lady Vane (who subsequently became Lady Londonderry) loved her for her kindness to all with whom she came in contact. I shall never forget her goodness and sympathy to me. She remained my friend until the day of her death and her sweet memory can never fade from my heart. So there it all was! I went up to London and was presented at Court, after which I returned to Warneford only to be dragged off on more and more journeyings which continued until I was about to stumble on my twentieth year.

CHAPTER III

In June 1869 we returned to England and alighted at Warneford for a short stay.

One morning my mother received a letter from one of her first cousins, who had, a year before, on the death of his uncle, the great Rajah Brooke, become the second Rajah of Sarawak. It was a touching epistle—reminding my mother of an occasion when, as children, they had met at the house of a friend and indulged in " childish pranks," my mother being his senior by two or three years. A parcel by the same post contained three or four large diamonds from her cousin's principality. The Sarawak revenues were at a low ebb and I learned several years later that the first Rajah Brooke had, a month or so before his death, written to his nephew advising him to proceed at once to England and marry his rich cousin, Mrs. de Windt.

Well, the playmate of former years was, on receipt of the letter (and the diamonds), invited by my mother to visit us at Warneford. He accepted the invitation and arrived there one afternoon while we were all having tea on the lawn.

He was evidently not accustomed to English country life. He wore a tall hat, a frock-coat and everything *en suite*. He was a good-looking man ; not very tall, but slim, with rather piercing grey eyes under bushy eyebrows, a very well-shaped nose, and a mouth depicting will and firmness, partly hidden by a grey moustache. His manner was very reserved, and in spite of " childish pranks " my mother and her cousin met each other as though they had just been introduced. My elder brother and I felt rather awed by him, but my younger brother, Harry, soon began to feel at home in his company.

The Rajah, on his side, appeared to feel attracted by Harry, who was then about fourteen, and they soon became good companions. I think that their friendship was probably based on their mutual love of adventure, the Rajah sensing that Harry would be interested in all he could tell him of Sarawak, and Harry feeling that this silent man could relate many a tale of head-hunting Dyaks in the far-off lands which he, already, was longing to visit. However it may have been, when the society of my mother, my elder brother and myself—not forgetting the aged spinsters— became too boring to the Rajah, he signed to Harry and together they disappeared down the long avenue, returning about an hour later deep in animated conversation, the tall hat still straight and firmly fixed on the great man's head.

In the evening there was whist, while my brother George and I took turns at the piano. Evidently, from what George and I had observed, the Rajah was a man of few words; especially during Harry's absence, he, on account of his youth, having been sent off to bed.　Imagine our surprise, therefore, to hear Harry next morning enthusiastically exclaim, " By Jove, he *is* a good talker; never stopped once in our walk.　He told me all about Sarawak—and the Dyaks—and the alligators and the snakes out there !　He *is* a good sort; a regular *man !*　I wonder whether he plays cricket."

Next day I was sent out riding with the potentate.　For miles and miles we cantered through fields, lessened our pace through green lanes, returning to the house after a two or three hours' ride *without having exchanged a word.*　On dismounting at the stables my companion made a bee-line for the lake, where he had espied Harry paddling a canoe.　Harry was delighted to see him and they talked and talked until it was time to dress for dinner.

So the days went on.　Silent rides with me in the afternoon, walks and talks with Harry be-tween-whiles, dinner and whist in the evening, when once more silence would reign supreme. The " childish prank " cousin remained with us ten days, after which our mother was preparing to drag us off on another of her pilgrimages abroad, this time to Innsbrück and the Tyrol. Realizing her cousin knew so few people in England, his parents living quietly at West Lackington, in Somersetshire, of which parish his father was vicar, my mother invited him to join our party and travel with us abroad. The Rajah fell in with this plan and we started on our way.

After stopping at many different places and hotels *en route*, we at length reached Innsbrück. By this time I had read the Rajah's book, *Ten Years in Sarawak*, in which he described in a modest and unassuming manner many of his adventures; fights against pirates and head-hunting Dyaks in which he had often risked his life for the protection of his uncle's subjects. A change had come over my feelings towards him. I was no longer disconcerted by his silence. I respected and admired him—as we all did—knowing how seriously he regarded his duty to his people and how great a help he had been to his uncle in the government of Sarawak.

At Innsbrück I found, to my great joy, that our private sitting-room in the hotel possessed a grand piano, and next morning I rose betimes, before the rest of the family were astir, to practise my music.

After playing over one or two of Chopin's Nocturnes, I was surprised to see the door open and the Rajah come into the room. He sat himself down on a chair near me and laid a rather grubby little piece of paper on the keys. It was scrawled over in pencil. " Read that," he said. I looked at him in some astonishment, picked up the paper and found these words:

"With a humble demean
If the King were to pray
That You'd be his Queen,
Would *not* you say *Nay ?* "

I read the words to myself and they made me
laugh. I went on laughing, for I imagined he
meant them for a joke and wanted to amuse me.
" Don't laugh," he said, rather crossly, " I mean
every word of it." I did not want to be rude,
but I knew not what to say. I had met so few
men and my heart was entirely free. No one
cared for me much at home except my brothers,
whom I deeply loved. My mother, poor darling,
was rather bored with me. I thought and
thought, remaining silent for some minutes.
Then " Do you really mean it ? " I said. " Do
you want to marry me ? " " I do," he replied
with more warmth than I had thought him
capable of. " What a lot of good you could do
in Sarawak ! My people would be your people.
Say ' yes ' and you will make me happy."

A picture came to my mind of my hitherto
useless days—and I wondered. It might be a life
of interest to me if I went out to Sarawak.
Although the Rajah was silent and reserved I
looked upon him as a hero and knew that he was
considered kind by all who came under his
influence. I thought of his book, his love for the
people of Sarawak and the devotion of his
subjects to him. My fingers wandered over the
keyboard. I look at him ; our eyes met ; his

were kind and grave. "Well," I said, "I *will*
say 'yes.'" Upon which he kissed my hand and
asked me not to tell my mother until our return
to Warneford. He then got up, went out of the
room, shut the door and disappeared. I looked
out of the window and saw him walking away
down the street. . . .

At breakfast my mother was considerably surprised when the waiter handed her a note from
the Rajah in which he announced that he was
leaving Innsbrück for England by the next train.

Although it all happened so many years ago I
remember thinking the whole proceedings very
strange. I do not imagine the poor dear man
could ever have been madly in love with me.
Realizing that he was unlikely to meet many
other girls in England, he thought, no doubt, that
I would do very well for Sarawak. On my side,
although I respected him and admired his achieve-
ments, I was never in love with him. I imagined
that in marrying him I might perhaps be of some
help to him and become of some use in the world
in which, up to that time, I had played so
insignificant a part.

In due course my mother, her train and myself
returned to Warneford. A day or two after our
arrival my mother received a letter from the
Rajah in which he told her that he had proposed
to me at Innsbrück and that I had accepted him.
My poor mother was taken aback—incredulous!
" Is it true," she said to me, " that he has asked

you to marry him and that you have said yes ? "
I stammered out something but did not say no.
" But how *can* you, Margaret ? You cannot
go out to Sarawak and live in the jungle in the
midst of savages and head-hunters ! " I said
nothing, for I felt there was nothing to say.
Next day the Rajah came to Warneford and a
stormy interview took place between the two, my
mother telling him that she could not allow the
match even if I *had* said yes ; I was only nineteen
and not of age. " But Margaret *promised* to
marry me," said the Rajah. Finally, I was sent
for, and as I came into the room my future
husband turned to me and said somewhat sternly,
" Did you, or did you not, say that you would
marry me ? " I, with the vision of my boring
home-life ever before me, said, " Yes, Charlie, I
did." " There ! You see ! " said he. " What
more do you want ? " To which my mother,
utterly bewildered, made no reply. He then
walked out of the room, banging the door behind
him, and went back to London.

My poor mother became very harassed in mind.
I do not think she greatly objected to my marrying
her " prank cousin." She knew him to be
honourable and high-minded, and feeling herself
unequal to coping further with the situation, she
gradually came to offer no further opposition to
the marriage. Indeed, after she got used to the
idea she began quite to *wonder* when she received
many letters of disapproval from her numerous

aunts and uncles, and especially from her cousin, Lady Vane, who considered the match an undesirable one both for the Rajah and myself owing to the disparity in our ages and also the uncertainty of an existence in a totally uncivilized country on the other side of the world.

However, the silent determination of the Rajah to marry me worked itself out according to his wish, as silent determinations so often do. So it came to pass that on the 28th of October, 1869, when I had only just attained my twentieth year, our marriage took place at Highworth Church. A few friends and neighbours were present at the ceremony, but no great-aunts, great-uncles or cousins; even the Rajah's father and mother remained away.

The wedding breakfast over, we got into the carriage to drive to Swindon station to catch the train for Exeter, where we were to stay the night. When the moment came for me to take leave of my two dearly-loved brothers I broke down completely, and was driven away from the door in a paroxysm of tears, my husband by my side. Not very complimentary to him, poor man! But I could not help myself. He said nothing, however, and I cried and cried until we reached the station.

My mother, with kindly forethought, had engaged a private compartment for us, feeling certain that such a proceeding would never have crossed the Rajah's mind. Arrived at the station, he went to the bookstall and bought *The Times* and *Punch*. He installed me in one corner of the carriage with *Punch* to read, settled himself in another corner and became deeply immersed in his newspaper until we reached Exeter.

There he had engaged rooms in quite a good hotel. We arrived just in time for dinner. The Rajah summoned the waiter and told him to bring us food. " Dinner, sir ? " the man said. " Oh, no," was the answer—" too expensive. Grilled legs of pheasants, bread-and-butter, tea and a half-bottle of sherry will do very well." A nasty sloppy sort of meal, I thought ! I ate bread-and-butter and drank tea, my husband partaking of the grilled legs and two small glasses of sherry. Oh dear ! It was all very dull and very queer.

The next morning the Rajah decided to drive to " Burrator," the small house in Devonshire left him by his uncle, where we were to spend our honeymoon. My French maid, Adrienne, who had been with me about six years, and my husband's valet—a Malay whom he had brought with him from Sarawak—were despatched in a bus with our luggage. The Rajah, preferring that we should make the journey by cab, engaged a modest vehicle drawn by a single, and rather elderly, horse. We left Exeter at midday and, about an hour later, as we were going through Crediton, I began to feel hungry and tentatively suggested an inn and some lunch. " Inns are no good," replied my spouse. " The food is always beastly; we'll be able to get some biscuits at almost any shop." Accordingly, the cab was drawn up at the first baker's, my husband jumped out and, throwing five shillings on the counter, said "Captain's biscuits," having probably made acquaintance with them during his naval career. The five shillings had hardly jingled its way into the till before bags and bags of biscuits were loaded into the cab. The Rajah sat and munched his biscuits, taking it all as a matter of course, but as far as I was concerned his large purchases had been in vain, for I could not eat them. Can anyone now living remember the nastiness of Captain's biscuits?

After what seemed to me a very long drive we reached "Burrator," a charming little abode standing on a low hill, surrounded by grassy lawns and trees gracefully curtseying themselves into a shallow stream whose waters, gurgling over rocks and pebbles, made gentle music by day and night. The place was full of memories of the late Rajah. It had been presented to him by his admirers in England, and there he had settled down to enjoy the last years of his life.

Two devoted servants of his, a Mr. and Mrs. Saul, were kept there as caretakers, and welcomed us as only such old and trusted retainers can. Mrs. Saul, who acted as cook and housekeeper, had prepared an early dinner which she duly announced, and the Rajah and I walked into the dining-room. In the middle of the table stood a small but beautifully decorated wedding cake, charmingly garnished with artificial orange-blossoms and white roses. " Oh, what a pretty cake ! " I cried, but the Rajah looked at it disapprovingly and said, " Quite unnecessary and very expensive." This remark caused the tears to spring to Mrs. Saul's eyes. " Oh, sir ! Oh, Rajah ! " she sobbed. " It was bought with my own money as a welcome to your young bride ! " The Rajah sat down to dinner and said nothing. I also sat down and said nothing ; but after dinner, when my husband was reading his paper, I found my way into the kitchen and gave the poor kindly soul a beautiful lace handkerchief, one of a specially lovely dozen my mother had given me in my trousseau. Mr. and Mrs. Saul became good friends of mine and I was greatly grieved when I heard some years later that they had both died.

My existence at " Burrator " was certainly by no means a whirl of gaiety. One day some neighbours of ours, Sir Massey and Lady Lopes, called. They were giving a ball at their place, " Marristow," and had come to invite us to stay the night with them and be present at the dance. The Rajah declined the invitation on the grounds that he had asked his mother and sister to come and stay with us and therefore could not leave the house. " Besides," he said to me after the kind people had left, " I don't want you to go to balls. You are never to dance round dances. I could never allow another man's arm round my wife's waist! And as for low gowns—don't ever let me see you wearing any such garments!" I felt greatly disappointed. I had learned dancing in Paris as a child, and in our sporadic stays at Vienna I had attended one or two balls with my mother, dancing with delightful Austrian partners to the strains of the great Johan Strauss's band. In Paris and London too I had been to a few balls and I *dearly* loved to valse. My spirits sank. But I tried to console myself as best I could by thinking that in Sarawak dances could never take place.

After a few days at " Burrator " the Rajah seemed to take more interest in life. He bought himself a couple of hunters and had my own hunter and another riding horse of mine brought over from Warneford. He also bought two small black untamed ponies. These ponies were harnessed to a little carriage and my husband became quite merry over the difficulty we had in piloting them through the narrow Devonshire lanes.

One day he made me drive them. I found them very hard to steer but did my best. All went fairly well until we came to a low wall with a ditch on either side. The road at this point was particularly narrow, and suddenly the ponies wheeled round and tried to jump the wall, with the result that the pony carriage turned over on its side and my husband and I found ourselves sprawling in the ditch, I still holding on to the reins. "Rather a narrow squeak, that!" said the Rajah, as he got up and proceeded to help me to my feet and disentangle me from the reins. "Great fun!" he said cheerily, "wasn't it?" He then told me to stay by the ponies and trap while he went to "Burrator" to get help from the village. In less than an hour he reappeared, accompanied by two or three yokels. The pony carriage, which, curiously enough, had not been much damaged, was pulled out of the ditch, the ponies were re-harnessed and my husband, jumping in, pleasantly invited me to come along and be driven home. He seemed quite astonished that I should prefer to *walk* back rather than risk a recurrence of the ponies' skittishness. All that evening he was very gay, saying what fun we had had; and how he meant to teach "these little devils" to behave in harness. At that time the Rajah was hardly ever known to buy well-mannered ponies or horses, saying that he rather liked their wildness at first and enjoyed taming them. Riding and driving were his favourite pastimes at "Burrator."

When his mother and sister came to stay with us I was left alone with them while he went off hunting and riding all day long. One day at luncheon I was feeling very fed-up with their company, as neither mother nor daughter made the slightest effort to talk. "I think I'll go out for a short ride this afternoon," said I. "I must tell them to saddle my horse." "*Your* horse!"

said the Rajah's mother to me severely. " Remember, young lady, that nothing is yours but your wedding ring." I am sorry to say that my reply was not in the best of taste. " If that is the case, Aunt Emma " (she was my great-aunt by marriage), " I shall appear to-night at dinner with nothing on but my wedding ring!" Tableau! Not another word was spoken by either lady throughout the afternoon. . . .

Christmas came and went. Time dragged rather heavily with my husband and myself at " Burrator." The Rajah hated Christmas festivities—the giving and receiving of presents, the greetings, the yule-tide fare—and I had to fight quite a hard battle in order to procure for the servants their turkey and plum pudding on Christmas Day.

On January 1st my mother sent me a cheque for £100, my quarter's allowance, my marriage settlements having guaranteed me £400 a year during her lifetime, whilst she had left me £800 a year in her will. I did not know what to do about the cheque, as hitherto my mother, in her lofty disregard for money, had flung bank-notes at me galore here and there at odd times. So I went to my husband, whom I found in a very good temper, having just sold my two horses for £150. I handed him the cheque, asking him to get it cashed for me as I wanted some money for myself. " What do you want money for ? " he asked. " That money " (£250) " comes in quite usefully for the extra expenses of our marriage, which would otherwise fall on the Sarawak treasury, and it will help pay your passage out." "But can't I have any of it, Charlie?" I asked, somewhat disappointed at the Sarawak treasury's requirements. "By and by we will see, but don't bother about it now!"

Poor dear, he had not the remotest idea that he was behaving in rather an extraordinary manner, nor had he the foggiest notion of the way in which Englishmen treated their wives. *His one and only thought was the prosperity of Sarawak.* He had married me, firstly and lastly, because I was young and very healthy and what he wanted above everything was an heir. He had lived for so many years in Sarawak that his ideas were Eastern. In his eyes his wife had no separate entity but was part of himself—his property—and he was firmly determined that anything belonging to him should never be a serious expense to the State.

I cannot endure rows, so I let him have his own way. We left London and stayed a few days at Boulogne to say good-bye to my mother and brothers, they having been detained in that town owing to the sudden illness which had overtaken my mother on her way back to England. None of us realized that her illness was so serious. She died in Boulogne a month after we had sailed from Marseilles, and a short time after our arrival at Sarawak the news of her death reached us. . . .

CHAPTER IV

BUT I had better tell something of our voyage out. We embarked at Marseilles on board a P. and O. liner. By that time I was expecting an infant, and as the weather from there to Alexandria was stormy, the sea frightfully rough and I a bad sailor, I became seriously ill. The ship's doctor attended me day and night, for I was feverish nearly all the time. My English maid whom I was taking out with me was obliged to remain in her cabin owing to sea-sickness and was of not the slightest use. The stewardess was angelic in her ministrations, and I shall never forget how wonderfully solicitous and kind my husband was to me. He was supremely good, and I felt more grateful to him than I could say. The voyage, as far as Singapore, left very little impression on my mind. It seemed to me one long nightmare of discomfort, monotony and sea-sickness. But I do quite vividly recall how, on one occasion when I felt a little better (or rather a little less ill!), my husband took me into the saloon to one of the concerts, thinking to cheer me up. The programmes of these concerts, I was told, bore a striking similarity to each other. A youth, on his way to a clerkship at Hong Kong, favoured the company with " Il Balen " from Verdi's " Trovatore." His voice was throaty and his rendering uncertain, he being accompanied by a nervous though well-intentioned spinster on her way to a prospective husband in the East. They were succeeded by a gentleman, returning to his business somewhere in the Malay Archipelago, who " obliged " with his one and only recitation, " Ocean ! Thou Mighty Monster ! " after which I decided that I had been sufficiently cheered up for one evening and returned to my cabin.

When we reached Alexandria I began to revive. In those days one had to journey by train from there to Suez. One morning early we boarded the boat at Suez which was to take us to Singapore. We stayed a night off Aden, spent a few hours at Point de Galle and threaded our way through the Malayan Archipelago to Singapore. I shall never forget my first impression of the exquisite beauty of tropical lands ! But I had no one with whom I could share my rapture. It sank into my innermost being, where, to my great joy, it has remained to this day.

How I loved to watch the porpoises that flumped and flopped around the vessel as she steamed along so calmly under the gentle April skies—the season of the fine monsoon. The flying-fish, too, like shimmering silver butterflies of the summer seas, as they darted and flew over the placid waters. . . .

Doctor Chambers, the new Bishop of Sarawak,

and his wife were on board our boat on their way out. He succeeded Bishop MacDougall, famous in the history of Sarawak for his devotion to the great Rajah and for the work he had done for the people. Sometimes, as I would be standing on deck drinking in the beauty of the exquisite scene, Mrs. Chambers would come up to me. " Lovely, isn't it ? " she would say. " Don't you think so ? "

One morning about eleven o'clock we reached Singapore and dropped anchor in the harbour, distant about four miles from the town. An aide-de-camp from Sir Harry Orde, Governor of Singapore, and a clerk sent by Sir Benson Maxwell, then Chief Justice of the Straits Settlements, boarded our steamer and presented my husband with letters offering us hospitality during our stay at Singapore. This placed my husband in a dilemma, as Sir Harry Orde and Sir Benson Maxwell, though both personal friends of the Rajah, were in direct opposition to each other and their inimical attitude was well known to all the residents. My husband therefore judged it better to decline both invitations as tactfully as possible and to take rooms in a good hotel in Singapore. His Sarawak agent, Mr. Read, who had come on board to receive us, made all necessary arrangements and we put up at the hotel. There I found beautiful baskets of flowers from Lady Orde and Lady Maxwell and charming greetings from those two delightful women, whose friendship was dear to me till their death and whose memory I still cherish.

My health was not good at that time owing to the natural consequences of matrimony. The banquet offered us at Government House was so grand that it somewhat frightened me, although their Excellencies were kindness itself, and the Sunday I spent at the Maxwells' beautiful house at Tanglin was tiring in the extreme notwithstanding the charming reception we were accorded by our hosts.

One evening of our three days' stay at Singapore stands out in my mind. I found it highly disconcerting. The Rajah's agent, Mr. Read, invited us to dine. I was the only lady present, the other guests being some ten or twelve men belonging to the different mercantile companies who had business in the Straits. Conversation had flagged during dinner, and afterwards the men all smoked horrible Manila cigars, partook freely of brandies-and-sodas and reclined, both feet up, on long bamboo couches placed about the room, my husband and I seated formally on two arm-chairs in the midst of the recumbent guests. I must say that terrible dinner-party did not make a very favourable impression on me.

Next morning we went on board the Rajah's yacht, the " Heartsease," which had arrived in the harbour to take us on the final stage of our journey. I then saw the Sarawak flag for the first time! That flag soon to become so dear to my heart, with its dark blue and red cross spread over a pale yellow ground. As the Rajah stepped on deck his standard, his personal emblem, was run up the mainmast. I felt very grand.

The captain, a good-looking young man, was brought up to be presented to me. Also the Sarawak doctor who had been sent with kindly consideration by the Resident, Mr. Crookshank, to take care of me during the forty-eight-hours passage from Singapore to Sarawak. The vessel moved off; I was shown to our state cabin, a roomy and comfortable one with bathroom attached, where, after my maid had undressed me, I—according to my usual procedure at sea —retired to my bunk, never leaving it until a succession of jolts followed by the smooth motion of the yacht told me that we had crossed the bar and reached calm water—the Sarawak river. Sea-sickness had come to an end!

I sprang up and looked out of the port-holes. Towards the north I saw a large expanse of sand strewn over with great brown boulders; a few cottages roofed with what looked like straw were scattered here and there. Some men, women and children were moving about on the sand, while others were jumping in and out of canoes, paddling up and down the river. Further inland, a great mountain, forest-clad up to the peak, refreshed my eyes with its green beauty after the long monotonous days at sea. On the other side of the vessel I noticed that the land was very flat and covered with trees which appeared to have their roots in the water. The glimpse of it all made me long to see it better. I bathed and dressed at once, and, feeling wonderfully restored, went up on deck, where I found my husband and Dr. Houghton silently smoking Manila cheroots after their early tea. They rose to greet me, the doctor pulling forward a bamboo couch. "You had better lie down," he said, and I forthwith flopped on to it, the two men relapsing into silence.

"How lovely it is, Charlie," I said. "Trees everywhere! And that glorious mountain! Can we go up it some day?" "Better try!" said my husband grimly. "That mountain is called Santubong!"

Presently one of our sailors came along the deck, and as he was about to pass the Rajah and myself he bent double and groped himself by. "Oh, the poor man!" said I. "He's ill! He must have a bad stomach-ache!" "Stomach-ache!" retorted my lord and master; "Malays always do that when they pass us. It's their way of showing respect." I felt somewhat squashed and again we relapsed into silence.

The next thing that met my view was a large mud flat, as yet uncovered by the incoming tide. On this I saw what I imagined to be some great trunks of trees. The next moment one of these suddenly came to life, reared aloft a huge horrible head and, with widely opened jaws, flumped into the river! "Oh, Charlie, look!" I cried in horror. "Can these muddy stumps be real crocodiles?" "Of course they're crocodiles," said "Charlie." "What else could they be?" "Of course," said the doctor. Silence again!

On we glided through reach after reach of densely wooded land, the banks becoming higher and the vegetation more varied: leafy palms, like green diadems, crowning the forest here and there. At one point the depth of the channel compelled us to hug the shore. Wonders will never cease, I thought, for there, jumping and swinging from branch to branch, I saw crowds of little monkeys, who, by their darting beady eyes, their chattering and grimacing, plainly showed us that they resented our intrusion.

"Oh, Charlie!" I cried in delight. "Just *look* at the darlings! Are they apes or monkeys?" "Monkeys, of course," said my husband. "Monkeys, of course," echoed the doctor. Silence once more! By this time I could not help noticing how the doctor seemed to model himself on the behaviour and manner of the Rajah, adopting his silences, echoing his remarks and even imitating his gestures. I discovered later that all my husband's officials did the same.

Now and then in a clearing we would see a few thatched cottages. On the river we met several covered canoes being paddled along by solitary males. They paid no attention whatever to the "Heartsease" as she steamed by. "They don't seem to take much notice of your return," I remarked to the Rajah. " Oh no," he replied. " Malays are not demonstrative in that way."

I thought of my childhood home in France and of how the dear French people would manifest their joy on my parents' return home to Epinay after even a short absence. I had, indeed, I felt, come into a different world.

Finally we arrived at a bend of the river, on the right bank of which, on the top of a hill, stood the Fort. A puff of smoke was seen ; this was followed by a loud report. They were firing a salute ! Then I saw the Sarawak flag flying from the top of a mast on a building near by. On a low hill on the opposite bank stood a good-sized white-washed bungalow, below which, by the water's edge, ran a street of picturesque shops which composed the Chinese bazaar. This was the principal thoroughfare of the town. Moored close to the shore were all sorts of odd craft— Chinese junks, Malay schooners, barges and canoes. Looking back again, across the river, I made out a small landing-stage on which were groups of Europeans and Malays, while on the top of the road leading from it stood the Residency, which was occupied at that time by Mr. and Mrs. Crookshank.

Mr. Crookshank was first cousin to my mother and my husband. He had been many years in Sarawak in the time of Sir James Brooke, and thoroughly understood the people. For this reason he had been left in charge of the principality during my husband's absence in England.

We anchored in mid-stream, whereupon the large and sumptuous state barge came alongside to take us ashore. It was manned by some twenty Malays with paddles. These men looked quite imposing in their white uniforms and embroidered caps. We descended into the barge and a few well-directed strokes of the paddles brought us to the landing-stage.

The Resident, Mr. Crookshank, and his wife were there to receive us together with Mr. and Mrs. Helms. Mr. Helms was the Sarawak agent of the Borneo Company. With them were Mr. St. John, Treasurer of Sarawak, and several gentlemen belonging to the Rajah's staff. By far the most impressive were four Malay chiefs, members of the Rajah's government, in their long flowing silken robes and beautiful turbans. It was a scene of brightness and gaiety, the people having gone to some trouble to give a good welcome to their Rajah and their Ranee. Bunting and paper streamers were to be seen everywhere and fire-crackers were being let off in all directions. Suddenly, from out of the others stepped a thin, somewhat elderly Malay holding a huge umbrella of yellow satin which he unfurled and held over my husband's head. The Rajah then led the way, the Resident offered me his arm, the rest of the company formed themselves into a sort of procession and we proceeded on foot up the narrow path that led to the Residency. At this point I ought to explain that we were to stay for a few days with Mr. and Mrs. Crookshank until the newly-built Astana (or palace) on the same side of the river was made ready for our reception. Although the building was completed the furniture had not yet arrived from England.

On reaching the Residency and before proceeding to luncheon, the attendant company were presented to me. How I loved the Hadjis, who touched their heads and their hearts in turn as they bowed beautifully and courteously before me. The Europeans left me somewhat cold. They were all very deferential to the Rajah but seemed inclined to ignore me. I had met Mr. and Mrs. Crookshank on a visit they had paid to my mother in Wiltshire a few years previously, when they were home on leave from Sarawak. I admired her intensely, both for her beauty and for her brave steadfast character. Not very tall, she had a slim and graceful figure, an exceedingly pretty face with small delicate features and large lovely brown eyes, while her dark hair, smooth and abundant, when unbound fell nearly to her feet. She and her husband had met and fallen in love in England and she had followed him out to Sarawak on his return there. Early in their marriage, when she was only seventeen, she had nearly met her death during the time of the Chinese insurrection, which was such a menace to Sarawak. Refusing to leave her husband's side, she had been exceedingly courageous and was greatly respected. She was also much liked for her kindness and hospitality to all the Rajah's English officials. Up to the time of my arrival Mrs. Crookshank had been the first lady in Sarawak. Can one be surprised, therefore, if at the back of her gentle mind she, a woman of thirty-three, should feel just a tiny bit annoyed that I, a young girl, "just out of the school-room" as she rather inaccurately phrased it, should take the place she had come to regard as hers?

Never shall I forget that first official luncheon. How strange and forlorn I felt and how I longed for someone who would stick up for me!

When luncheon was over we three ladies left the men downstairs and established ourselves upstairs in the drawing-room. Mrs. Crookshank and Mrs. Helms then proceeded to discuss the new Bishop Chambers and his wife. "Horrid woman!" said Mrs. Crookshank. "She will want to go in to dinner before me. However," she continued in a serene but very decided voice, "my husband is the Rajah's prime minister, and prime ministers' wives always take precedence over bishops' wives." Then, turning to me, she said with rather a forced smile, "And what are *you* to be called? I hear that Mrs. Chambers has put it about that it would be wrong to call you 'Ranee.'" "Why?" I said, meekly enough, but remembering the poem at Innsbrück in which the Rajah had asked me to become his queen. " Because, dear, you would not like people to imagine that you were a *black* woman ! " " But Sarawak people are *not* black," said I, remembering the four dear Datus, their courtesy and politeness on being presented to me. " I should rather *like* being taken for a Malay." "Well!!!" exclaimed both the ladies. And there, for the time, the matter rested.

CHAPTER V

When our furniture had arrived from England
and had been arranged in the Astana we concluded our stay at the Residency, and after taking
leave of Mr. and Mrs. Crookshank took up our
abode at the Palace. I was naturally glad to feel
that at last we were settled in our own home.
And a very lovely home I thought it. The
Astana was built on a low green hill that over-
looked the river and formed a promontory between two streamlets that emptied themselves into
the main channel. It was built in the form of
three bungalows, supported by square brick
pillars some twenty feet above the ground. The
low-spreading roof gave shade to the interior.
The largest bungalow stood in the centre and
contained the reception-rooms and dining- and
drawing-rooms, which were large, lofty and cool.
The smaller bungalows each contained two large
bedrooms with bathrooms attached. We occupied the western bungalow, the eastern one being
reserved for the use of visitors. A large verandah
was one of the pleasantest features of this delightful abode, and on it were passed some of the
happiest hours I spent in Sarawak.

A beautiful garden led down to the landing-stage amid green lawns and grassy walks, bordered and shaded by bamboos and betel-nut palms under which grew great clumps of red and white lilies. Exotic flowers bloomed everywhere, gardenias, tuberoses, cape jessamine, filling the air with their perfume, and at the side and back of the Astana many tree-bordered paths led to the mysterious depths of luxuriant forest which stretched for miles around.

I found our bathrooms the most original and surprising apartments. A short flight of wooden steps led down to them from the bedrooms. They were very dark, having no windows, but being lit only by rays of light through narrow chinks close to the ceiling. The floors were tiled and had little runways to carry off the water. This was all very well, but where were the *baths*? There were none, at least not the baths to which Europeans are accustomed. Sarawak was (and is) decidedly primitive in its methods of bathing. A large stone tank, or cistern, is to be found in the corner of these vault-like rooms. This is kept filled with water by the Chinese, who carry it up from the river. Above the tank hangs a basket made of Nipa palm leaves, and this is the procedure. You stand on a stone slab, dip the basket into the cistern and, having filled it, dash the water over yourself, soaping yourself at intervals. Quite strenuous but very refreshing, I found, after I had become expert at wielding the water-basket or dipper. I used to resort to these baths as a restorative many times a day, much as Englishwomen at home resort to their never-failing cup of tea.

The Malays are a people who are always popping in and out of water, bathing five or six times daily in the rivers, and teaching their children to swim almost as soon as they are old enough to walk.

. . . . . .

The English society in Kuching that year (June 1870) was composed of Bishop and Mrs. Chambers, the Resident and his wife—Mr. and Mrs. Crookshank—Mr. and Mrs. Helms (Mr. Helms besides being Agent to the Borneo Company Limited also acted as British Consul at Sarawak). The unmarried men were Mr. Oliver St. John, Treasurer, Major Rodway, who commanded the small contingent of Native troops in Kuching, and two or three young men who occupied less important posts on the Rajah's staff. The population of the small capital then numbered about 30,000, including Malays, Hindus, Chinese, etc.

The name by which I was to be known gave the English ladies at Sarawak no small concern. For my part, it gave me little thought. I was the Rajah's wife, therefore it was quite clear to me that I was the Ranee (such a pretty-sounding name, I thought!). His people were my people, and indeed I loved them from the first. That was all that mattered to me. As for my husband, he was immersed in governmental affairs and had little time to spare for the bickerings of ladies to whom he hated to have to lay down the law, disliking intensely any behaviour that savoured of pomposity or self-aggrandisement. Was I not his wife, part of himself, belonging entirely to him ? That was enough, surely—anything else could wait !

At last one day, quite suddenly, my title was bestowed on me, and by a very humble bestower —a medicine bottle ! A short time after our arrival at the Astana, a slight ailment necessitated the attendance of Dr. Houghton, who promised to send me a tonic that evening. The package containing the medicine bottle fell into my husband's hands. The label bore the name " Mrs. Brooke " in the doctor's own handwriting. The Rajah glared at the poor little bottle and wrathfully sent for Dr. Houghton. The time had come, he thought, to settle this matter once and for all and let his wishes be broadcast throughout his country. On the arrival of the doctor my husband pointed sternly to the label and said, " You must be singularly bereft of your senses if you think my wife can be addressed otherwise than as the *Ranee*. Take the thing away and address it properly." Without my having partaken of one dose, the bottle was speedily removed, the doctor returning later to present it to me with many apologies and its amended label. One must find one's way to lands far removed from

Europe to discover a medicine bottle invested with all the dignity of a Lord Chamberlain. Henceforth I became " The Ranee " to all the English residents, while the darling Malays went one better and insisted on calling me " Rajah Ranee."

However, the sayings and doings of the English society did not interfere with my healthy appetite or cause me sleepless nights. I grew to understand and agree with the Rajah's wish that I should not become too intimate with the English ladies at Kuching. " Let them say what they like," he said, " and don't talk too much," and, following his advice, we all got on very well.

More and more I came to admire the way in which my husband governed his country, always setting its interests before his own and planning for the betterment of his people. He was indeed their Rajah, protector and friend. Although I regretted that his manner was cold and reserved I knew how good and kind he was, and came to realize that in his position as ruler over an undemonstrative people he must never, never wear his heart upon his sleeve. Unfortunately for himself as well as for me, my husband was without a sense of humour, whilst I responded only too readily to the funny side of things, finding it at times almost impossible to suppress my sense of the ridiculous.

According to my husband's wish a certain time had to be devoted to social affairs, and he

approved of my suggestion that I should hold a
reception for our English friends once a week.
So every Tuesday afternoon the English ladies,
their husbands and the bachelor officials belonging
to the Rajah's staff came to tea at the Astana.   I
cannot say our conversation was ever very exciting, but they were all very amiable.   One thing
surprised me greatly ; they appeared to take little
or no interest in the affairs relating to the country,
but would wax quite enthusiastic when someone
would announce how, with great good fortune, he
had induced a small half-ripe strawberry to
appear on a plant he had brought from England !
With flowers it was just the same.   " Only think,"
another would say.   " You know the red geranium
shoots I brought from England ?   Well, I do
believe we shall be able to get at least four
blooms ! "   " Really ?   How splendid ! "   the
others would reply admiringly.   This in the
midst of the exquisite prodigality of the tropics.

They all wanted to be oh, so English ! whilst I
hankered after being oh, so Malay !

Now and again we would have dinner-parties,
one nearly the counterpart of the other, to which
the whole English community—some fifteen or
sixteen in number—would be invited.   After
dinner there would be music in the drawing-
room.   The Rajah, knowing my love for the
piano, had bought me an Erard, but alas ! a few
wet days would render one or two of its notes
mute and my manifestations on the instrument

would, in consequence, be somewhat marred! Happily, society in Sarawak was not highly critical. The music of the great Masters—even when played on a properly functioning piano!—would only have bored them. Several of our guests, however, could be depended upon to bring their songs (always the same) and thus contribute to the harmony of the evening. Even the Rajah would join in the fray! Mrs. Helms and the other ladies had given it as their profound conviction that he had a lovely tenor voice. The edict having gone forth, the Rajah would open the programme by singing with dignity and gravity " La Donna e Mobile " to his own, and apparently everybody else's, satisfaction. Poor darling, he never sang in tune, and once, when we were alone, I hazarded the opinion that a little practice in *solfège* might do him good. He stared at me blankly, then remarked in an offended tone that if I did not like his singing he would not sing any more. I hastily apologized, took back my words, nothing more was said, and " La Donna " remained on the programme at all our parties.

Truly, much is to be said in favour of the same programme pursuing its unerring course on the occasions of such social gatherings. Sarawak had never been known to falter or to fail! Desultory conversation filled in the interval between each item. One of the Borneo Company's agents was noted for his fine baritone voice and he would

ring out " The Village Blacksmith " to the delight
of his friends, rendering with great delicacy and
pathos the passage " It sounds to him like her
mother's voice singing in Paradise," at which
point the ladies could be relied upon to show their
appreciation by tiny sniffs and gentle pattings of
their eyes with their handkerchiefs. Our musical
programme always ended with our good doctor,
possessed of a tenor voice—" but not so good as
the Rajah's "—inquiring " Oh, don't you remember sweet Alice, Ben Bolt ? " . . .

After lemonade for the ladies and brandy-and-
soda for the men the guests would depart home-
wards, each expressing his, or her, appreciation
of the evening in his, or her, accustomed way.

Doubtless many people could be found who
would take exception to the sameness of our
gatherings, but on the whole they were comfortable. We all of us knew exactly what to
expect, and in the heat of such tropical evenings
a change of programme might have been unduly
exciting and bad for us !

The truth of the saying about a prophet being
without honour in his own country was borne in
upon me. My rôle was a modest one, for I had
only to supply the accompaniments, and though I
felt very pleased at the enjoyment of our guests
and the delight they evinced in listening to the
innocuous programme of songs, I was rather surprised (not being devoid of conceit !) that, in
spite of one or two dumb notes in the bass or

treble of our piano, caused by the damp climate, our guests never invited me to play a solo. Nor did I leave them in ignorance of my musical accomplishments but, being my own trumpeter, I dinned into their ears the fact that from my eighth birthday, right down my teens, musical celebrities had given me lessons and praised my performance. Arabella Goddard, Charles Hallé, Pauer—even that king among pianists, Thalberg, had taught me and spoken well of me, if you please! Alas! the Kuchingites failed to display any interest in my attainments and the musical evenings went on without any piano solo on my part. I, being inordinately pleased with my playing, could only pity them. Autre temps, autre mœurs! Thus runs the world away. . . .

CHAPTER VI

AND so the days went on, placidly and happily. At daybreak I would rise to watch my husband start out for his morning ride. After he had gone I would stay on the verandah watching the miracle of beauty which is sunrise in Sarawak. So long would I gaze, entranced, upon the scene, that I had often to hurry considerably over my toilet in order to be in time for the Rajah's return about eight o'clock. At that hour the Datus, those delightful Malay chiefs (my husband's ministers), would arrive at the Astana to escort the Rajah to the Court House across the river, where, assisted by Mr. Crookshank, he dispensed law and order to his subjects. Their departure from the Astana was most picturesque. As the Rajah stepped outside the porch, Subu would unfurl the large yellow state umbrella over his head and they would set forth. Behind His Highness walked his Malay ministers in their rich robes and beautiful turbans, they, in turn, being followed by the usual retinue of subordinate Malays. They looked to me so very biblical, those dear, kind, grave Hadjis, as they marched along with their slow and stately tread. I used to feel as though I had just taken leave of

Abraham, or Jacob, or Esau! Bless their hearts, they have all now left the world. Some day, who knows, I may find them in spirit to welcome me in the land beyond the sun. . . .

The Rajah returned from the Court House at noon, when breakfast was served, after which he rested, as is customary during the hottest hours of the day. At five o'clock we took tea together on the verandah. Then we would go for a paddle excursion up and down the river. At eight we dined in the enormous dining-room (so large and empty for two solitary souls!), waited upon by Talip, our butler, and four young Malay boys, their bare feet making their movements as silent as if they had been ghosts.

One morning, however, the even tenor of our days was disturbed by the arrival of a messenger from Mr. Skelton, the Resident at Sibu. He came with the news that the Fort had recently been attacked by a redoubtable and extremely troublesome Dyak chief, called Lintong, who, because of his head-hunting exploits, had been punished by the Government. Lintong, in revenge, had mustered several hundred of his tribesmen and set out from his mountain stronghold, down the river Rejang, to attack the Fort at Sibu, hoping to take it by surprise. But Mr. Skelton, with his well-drilled Native troops and Indian Sepoys, was ready for them, and no sooner was the Dyak fleet, with its torches, spears and war accoutrements, sighted on the river at dawn, than it met with a fusillade of shots from the Sepoys' rifles, whereupon Lintong and his warriors turned tail and made off helter-skelter back up the river, realizing no doubt that their optimism had been misplaced.

This uprising of Lintong's necessitated the Rajah's departure for the Sibu Fort to restore law and order, and next morning he went on board the " Heartsease " at daybreak. I accompanied him along the garden path and down the steps to the landing-stage. " Oh, Charlie," I implored, " do be careful, and promise me you won't get killed ! " " Get killed ! " was his reply ; " I'll be safer up at the Fort than if I were standing on the dome of St. Paul's." I thought this a very curious remark but decided that it was intended as a reassurance and therefore appeared to understand. Pondering it over later, I concluded that he was undoubtedly right. We said good-bye, and the ship's boat took him off to the yacht, which was anchored in mid-stream. As he stepped on board, his flag was hoisted to the main, the anchor weighed and the ship steamed its way past where I stood and disappeared round a bend of the river.

I went back to the Astana and sat myself down alone with a book on the verandah. I laid aside the book and looked about me. What an odd world I had come to, I thought, but I

must get accustomed to this new existence; with
its wars and rumours of wars, its head-hunting
expeditions and the Rajah suddenly chivied off
from pillar to post as a protection to his subjects
all over the country. "Uneasy lies the head
that wears a crown" among head-hunting subjects! At any rate, knowing nothing of such
matters, I felt very anxious for his safety, the
more so as I knew many days must elapse before
news could reach me from Sibu. In those days
of long ago, telegraphy was unknown in Sarawak, and the only means of communication between one district and another was by canoes
propelled by paddles, necessitating some forty-
eight hours' journey from Sibu to Kuching.
However, there it all was, and nothing I could
do would change matters. Better make the best
of things! And sitting in my chair on the
verandah, beauty pressed on me from all sides.

Far away towards the south the Singghi mountain range, blue as cobalt above the forest lands,
zigzagged its way across a paler blue sky. The
Matang range barring the sunset, also wooded
to the summit, loomed a darker blue. Near by,
on the opposite bank of the river, stood the
Chinese bazaar with its highly decorated houses
painted and adorned Chinese fashion, where the
Kuching population—Malays, Hindus, Land-
Dyaks and others—were busy buying provisions
for the day. English, Dutch, Malay schooners
and Chinese junks were anchored in the river

near the bazaar, and canoes large and small, roofed-in and otherwise, were being paddled to and fro. All around me in the Astana gardens small grey monkeys—called Wah-Wahs by the Malays—were singing their morning hymn. It sounded as though innumerable jugs of water were being poured down the branches of the trees. Fluttering about a shrub on the lawn covered with crimson blossoms, tiny birds, somewhat larger than dragon-flies, with feathers tinted all the colours of the rainbow, poked their beaks in and out of the trumpet-shaped blooms. They were so delicate, so gorgeous and so lovely! The flowers sent their perfume over the air. How beautiful it all was—mysterious, sweet, wonderful! The sky was blue and serene, the sun shining. Surely Almighty God was in a good temper!

At this point my musings were interrupted by the sight of a picturesque figure on the verandah. It was Talip, the butler. He had been in the service of the late Rajah for many years and at his death retained the position of butler at the new Astana. Honest, loyal and devoted was Talip to both his masters. Good-looking too, tall for his race, slim and well-built, with beautiful faithful eyes and not too squat at nose or too thick lips. Quite a dandy in his way. His handkerchief of yellow silk tied neatly and jauntily around his head, his yellow and black chequered sarong (yellow is the royal

colour) folded beautifully round his waist, setting
off to perfection his white drill coat and trousers.
He could speak a little English. Bowing low
and bending nearly double, which he did with
astonishing dignity and grace, he inquired with
deep respect if Rajah Ranee wanted anything.
"No, thank you, Talip," I replied, "but"
(indicating with a wave of my arms the lovely
scene around us) "isn't it all beautiful?" I
said, as well as I could in the few words of Malay
I had managed to pick up. Talip smiled and
seemed happy that I admired his country and
was trying to speak its language. He repeated
my words, then, after a pause, said, "If Rajah
Ranee want anything, Rajah Ranee tell Talip."
"Oh, trimakassi (thank you), Talip," I said,
"yes, I will." He doubled himself up again—
another smile—and departed. I felt that I had
found a friend. Now, it may seem odd to
sticklers for etiquette in England that the Rajah's
wife should feel that in her husband's native
butler she had found a friend, but I can only
say that that is how I *did* feel. At breakfast
that day as I entered the vast dining-room, feeling rather like a fly on a large mound of sugar,
Talip gave an example of his kindness and
thoughtfulness for me. He managed the household and arranged the meals, to my infinite
relief. I found that he had provided an extra
specially lavish and varied menu to console me
in my loneliness. There seemed to be no end

to the dishes he pressed me to partake of. Surely never had so many dainties and condiments been served with any curry! He even ran to pickled onions! I was truly thankful when the arrival of custard apples signified that the repast was about to end. Never shall I forget that meal.

My siesta that afternoon was a long one. Indeed it extended practically till next morning, for I felt certain that unless I remained in bed there would be no other way of escaping the dinner which I felt sure Talip would have devised for me.

.   .   .   .   .

At tea-time Mr. and Mrs. Crookshank often came to call. Mr. Crookshank, experienced in Sarawak affairs, made me understand that the Rajah was in no danger. Mrs. Helms came too, and whenever I was alone with her, she—being the mother of two young daughters, both born in Kuching—considered it her duty to advise me regarding my condition, as I was expecting an infant in a few months' time. She warned me as to the dangers which might arise owing to certain precautions not being attended to, and once or twice during her kindly admonitions I felt Death almost staring me in the face. Never mind! She meant well. As for me, being young and healthy and knowing nothing of birth arrivals, my nerves did not get the better of my optimism on the subject.

Mrs. Chambers never put in an appearance during the Rajah's absence, on account of a certain amount of friction having arisen between Church and State. This is what took place.

On a Sunday before the Rajah departed for Fort Sibu, Bishop Chambers preached his first sermon as prelate in Kuching Church. The Rajah was present as well as most of his officials. Mrs. Chambers, who, on account of her dominating character and her airs and graces, had been given the nickname of " Mrs. Proudie " by those who resented her patronage, had taken it upon herself to advise her lord and master on his first address from the pulpit. She evidently considered that new brooms should sweep clean. Thus it happened that so thorough was the new broom in its sweepings, and the Bishop in his denunciations of the Rajah's officials and their ways, that all present felt a fierce anger rising in their hearts. Although the Bishop impressed on them the burning desire he felt to bring his flock back to the fold and his congregation into leading better lives, the poor flock had really nothing to reproach themselves with, their lives having been quiet, simple and orderly. The Rajah himself was very much angered, and with good reason. The service over, he went his way home, and there and then wrote the Bishop a " what-for " letter, in which he also touched on the many services he and his officers had rendered to the S.P.G. But " Mrs. Proudie " was on the look-out and had made up her mind that the Bishop must remain—righly or wrongly—paramount in Church affairs. The episcopal answer, prompted by her, added fuel to the flames, with the result that, for the time being, Church and State in Sarawak were torn apart. Of course the Rajah was perfectly right to act as he did, but Mr. and Mrs. Crookshank, who much disliked " Mrs. Proudie," did their best to widen the breach and prevent the unpleasantness being cleared up. For three years the feud went on, and only came to an end when the Crookshanks left Sarawak to settle in England.

It is rather amusing but somewhat disconcerting to realize how the members of almost any community of English men and women settled in out-of-the-way places take pleasure in having rows with one another, especially those who are ignorant of the world, who know nothing of Society with a big S, and who, suddenly finding themselves in a remote land, imagine that they are Somebody. They are apt to become pompous and silly, and to be jealous of those who receive more attention than they, when they revel in picking quarrels with those who may be their superiors. I used to think, when I heard of all these quarrels going on around me, how futile they all were. Mrs. Chambers was not very amiable, but why should Mrs. Crookshank have tried to keep the " fire burning " and

utterly forget the wonderful Romance, the beautiful story that had come to pass, of Sarawak, its
first Rajah and the people who, through him,
were looking for guidance to the officials who
helped their Rajah in his wonderful task?

CHAPTER VII

However kind and charming the English ladies were to me, the days weighed somewhat heavily on my hands, and I began to wonder where all the Malay women were—the Datus' wives, sisters, cousins and aunts. Where had they hidden themselves? Without delving too deeply into the question of population—even that of Kuching —I could not help feeling certain that the Rajah's Malay officials must possess, somewhere, females who were responsible for their appearance in the world. So one day I sent for Talip. "Talip," I said, "I want to give a party. I want to invite all the Malay ladies of Kuching, old and young, to the Astana." When I had impressed on him that I wanted *all* the women to be included, Talip was eager to obey my orders, and in a masterly way carried out all arrangements as to invitations, catering, procedure and the like. The women were delighted at the prospect, and when the great day came and I beheld them assembled in our large dining-hall, I was charmed at the sight.

At the top of the hall Talip had placed a large and throne-like arm-chair for me. On this he had piled innumerable cushions, and on either side were set two uncushioned chairs for the wives of the four Datus. Talip had impressed upon me the importance of waiting until all the guests had assembled before I made my entrance, for, he said, " Rajah Ranee must never be waiting to receive her subjects." When they had all arrived, Talip came to my room to escort me to my place. As I slowly entered the hall, Talip walking before me with measured tread, the women seemed to me lovely, although I daresay many Europeans will wonder at my taste in beauty. But the large glowing dark eyes fringed with long silky lashes, the shining black hair, the gleaming polished skins of palest yellow, the small, slim, lissom bodies that moved with such easy grace, the tiny hands and feet of these women went a very long way to make up for the squat noses, thick lips and high cheek-bones, which marred what would otherwise have been almost perfect beauty.

The older and married women wore dark colours, and their sarongs, jackets, scarves and mantillas were more sombre than those of the maidens. This is because they are married and it would not be seemly for them to adorn themselves in any manner calculated to attract the attention of the male. But with young girls it is different, and their dress may be as brilliant and alluring as they can make it. In addition to their brightly coloured and embroidered garments, they, being virgins, may wear plaques of gold upon the breasts of their jackets. These, together with their golden ornaments of every description, produce a gorgeous effect that delights the eye, while the swishing of their silks and satins and the jingling of their many ornaments as they move about are like music to the ear.

Such was the sight on which I looked down from my improvised throne! As Talip's eye was more for effect than for comfort, he had piled so many cushions on the seat that, tall as I was, my feet would not have reached the floor had I attempted to sit on it. I occupied it as best I could, and I can't help saying that I managed to achieve the feat with a good deal of dignity.

The most important ladies present, the wives of the Datus (my husband's ministers), were then led up by Talip to be presented to me. They made lovely curtseys, bowing low before me and touching their foreheads and their hearts in turn. They then enfolded both my hands in theirs, after which they took their seats by my side. All the others did likewise, and by the time the ceremony was concluded I began to feel rather tired.

However, a break came, refreshments were handed round, and afterwards I began to grope my way into conversation with my subjects, with the aid of Marsden's Malay and English Dictionary and Talip, as interpreter, to help me out when I became too deeply involved. My first few halting words evoked a torrent of response from the four ladies beside me. This was altogether more than I could cope with, but Talip came to the rescue. " They say, Rajah Ranee, you are their father, their mother and their grandmother. They want to take care of you and to cherish you, but Datu Isa says that you are very young, so that she looks upon you as being also her child. When the Rajah is not at your side, if you are sad, send for the Malay women and they will help to lighten your heart." I felt touched, and expressed my gratitude. Presently our conversation became less formal and we felt as though some bond united us all. We even indulged in one or two mild jokes. Then, after ceremonious leave-takings, they departed to their homes, to their men-folks, anxious no doubt to hear of the novel experience of their wives and daughters in meeting for the first time with their White Ranee. I returned to my room, the lamps were lit, and my little maid, Ima, was sitting in a corner, her back against the wall.

. . . . . .

I took such a fancy to the women's dress, so simple, cool and graceful-looking, that I made up my mind to wear it myself occasionally, when parties with the Europeans did not necessitate fashions from Bond Street or the Rue de la

Paix. Then of course I had to send for Talip. "Talip," I said, "I want you to give Ima some money to go over to the bazaar and buy me materials for a Malay dress." His face fell. "Rajah Ranee," he said, "how shall I find the money to buy the brocade, the gold, the rich ornaments for such a dress? Only the richest will do." "Not a bit of it, Talip," I replied; "that will come later. Some cotton, some ordinary washing silk and a cheap scarf will do quite well to go on with." It took a little time to get him reconciled to the idea of my simple attire, but I had my way, the materials were bought, and in a very few hours Ima's skilful fingers had fashioned them into a complete dress for me. I thoroughly enjoyed putting on the costume, so comfortable it was, the discarding of my stays, too, those mid-Victorian horrors of steel and whalebone worn by fashionable females of that era. In my cool garb I felt free, untrammelled and (greatest of all charms in my eyes) quite Malay!

On the return of the Rajah a few days later, when he saw me seated in my room in my humble Malay dress, a look of amusement came over his face. "Hallo! Quite settling down," he remarked with approval. "Yes, Charlie," I said. After which I seized the propitious moment to confess about my party. He appeared to be very pleased. Not one word of reproach, not one reflection on "the expense." Such manifestations, he evidently thought, were good for the country. He really approved of it all although he remained quite silent on the subject.

A few weeks later, Datu Isa, realizing how much the Malay dress appealed to me by my wearing it occasionally, came with the other Datu wives to present me with a beautiful sarong and scarf woven by themselves in golden thread. To this they added a dark blue satin jacket trimmed with golden plaques, and with rows of golden buttons on the sleeves. They had obtained from Mecca a lovely gauze veil for the head, and this completed the charming costume. I was very grateful for the gift, and I asked Datu Isa and the other ladies to help me put it on. Datu Isa then took command and ventured a few remarks on the occasion. " We have thought much, Rajah Ranee, about what your dress should be, and we feel that as you are the wife of our Rajah you must have gold on it so as to make it beautiful." Nothing could have given me greater happiness than this gift from our people and to know the care they had bestowed on every detail of its fashioning. But there was just one drawback concerning my wearing it. It was the extreme length of the skirt, worn completely covering my feet, so that walking about in it was a somewhat difficult problem. Unconsciously I gave a little hitch to the skirt, when Datu Isa exclaimed, " Oh no, Rajah Ranee ; as the wife of our Rajah your feet must not be seen. You are not supposed to walk at all, for as you are our Ranee you must be waited on and your every want supplied by your attendants." Datu Isa's daughter-in-law, Daiang Sahada, who was about my own age, and who was present at the time, came to me and whispered, "Don't mind much about what she says; we all know you can do no wrong, so wear the dress as you like. She is old, and enjoys giving lessons to everybody about everything, and we let her have her way." I pretended to agree with Datu Isa's views, but went on in my own way, and when I did wear the beautiful dress the old lady seemed to be quite content although the tips of my golden slippers could be seen as I walked about the room.

CHAPTER VIII

My husband had brought back with him Mr.
Harry Skelton, the Resident at Fort Sibu, who,
with his well-drilled Native troops and Indian
Sepoys, had so ably defended the Fort and sent
Lintong and his rebel men flying back to their
fastness up the river. A punitive expedition con-
sisting of non-head-hunting Dyaks commanded
by Malays had been sent by the Rajah to attack
the offending Lintong's village, raze it to the
ground, and destroy the rice farms. They had,
of course, strict orders to spare all women and
children. Lintong was taken prisoner and
brought to Fort Sibu. Such were the methods
employed by the first two Rajahs to settle the
affairs of their rebel subjects. In order to suppress the risings of the Dyak tribes whose sporting instincts led them to attack their more peaceful neighbours and carry off a head or two, it
was necessary that they, in turn, should be dealt
with as I have described. When their villages
and crops had been destroyed, the rebel tribes
were forced to establish themselves at a spot
below the rapids where, the stream being navigable, the Rajah's gunboats and the comparative
proximity of the Fort could coerce them into

proper behaviour. Lintong, not content with his head-hunting exploits, had gone further than any rebel chief and had actually attacked the Rajah's Fort. Therefore he was made prisoner and shipped aboard the " Heartsease " to Kuching. His captivity was not a severe one. He was put in charge of the Police, sent to stay with those who would be responsible for his whereabouts and made to see the error of his ways. On the whole, I imagine he spent rather a good time. His new neighbours pointed out to him that cutting off people's heads was really not so important after all, and that he would be much happier and better off to live peaceably at the head of his tribe below the rapids, where—just so long as he was law-abiding—he might live unmolested and farm his lands to his heart's content. This humane method of dealing with offenders had proved highly successful and many a hitherto cut-throat group of Dyaks had thus been turned into supporters of the Government and won over to suppressing other head-hunters.

To return to Lintong. He came to see me once or twice. Rather shifty-looking, I thought, with his small dark furtive eyes. He was well built and moved gracefully, as all Dyaks do. Shabbily dressed, his chawat (or waistcloth) was made of bark, and he was naturally not allowed to wear his head-dress of feathers which denoted to the Dyak world that he had appropriated human heads. No, Lintong was not smartly dressed when I saw him. On the one or two occasions when he walked with me in the garden of the Astana, he talked a great deal, but as I could not speak the Dyak language, which is different from Malay, I was not able to understand a word he said. I saw, however, that he was trying to make himself pleasant and could not help feeling rather amused. The *débâcle* at Sédan had then just taken place and Napoleon III was a prisoner in Germany. I would think to myself sometimes, " I don't suppose Napoleon III goes out walking with the Empress Augusta in the Royal garden in Berlin ! . . . But, after all," I would say, " isn't there a certain analogy ? Me, the reigning Rajah's wife, walking in the garden with Lintong, a prisoner of war ! Augusta, Empress of Germany, and Napoleon, ci-devant Emperor of the French ! Of course one may sniff in a superior manner at the disparity in importance of our respective countries, but if Napoleon had only governed his people with a firm hand, and the Emperor of Germany been possessed of half the sense of Sarawak's Rajahs, Napoleon could have run back to France much as Lintong will go back to his tribe, and peace be restored without all the trouble, muddle and fuss. . . . But there it all is, and I do not suppose that there will be many who will agree with me ! "

The methods I have just pictured by which

the two Rajahs strove to eradicate head-taking in Sarawak were, as I have said, most successful, and it is very seldom that recurrences are heard of nowadays. In an open hand-to-hand fight for the Government the combatants are still allowed to carry off their enemies' heads and take them home as war trophies, but as both sides are imbued with the same idea they know exactly what to expect and are quite ready for any emergencies of the kind! After all, who is there that would not prefer warfare waged in such a way—a swift, clean cut that chops off one's head—to the bestial cruelties now indulged in in war between European countries, where non-combatants in cities—women and children —are in danger of death by torture through gas poisoning, bombs and other " civilized " modern devilries ? But, luckily, in Sarawak no money is to be made by company promoters who invent hideous deaths for belligerents of any nationality, including their own.

Now, to come back to Mr. Skelton. He had been nearly four years in the Rajah's service, having joined when about twenty-four years old. As he had proved himself a competent officer the Rajah had recently appointed him to his present Residency at Sibu. Like all the Rajah's officials, he was devoted to his Chief. He told me in confidence (why ?) that he thought my husband was the most wonderful man he had ever met, whereupon I, in wifely pride, patted him on the

shoulder and said " Good boy ! " He was very
tall and fair, with charming blue eyes, and—
thank goodness !—he could *talk*! Yes, from the
first we got on splendidly and speedily became
friends. We had many interesting talks together
when the Rajah was at the Court or taking his
rides in the cool of the evening after tea, and I
found that he could teach me many things about
the country. We got hold of a map of Sarawak,
as it was in those days. " Look," he would say,
" we are at Kuching. You know all about the
river from Santubong to the capital. See here,
if you get into a canoe and go right up the river,
you will arrive at the country of the so-called
Land-Dyaks. In olden days the Land-Dyaks
were given to taking heads, but although these
people still keep the heads as ancestral trophies,
they imagine said heads to have lost their virtue.
These Land-Dyaks are supposed to be the abo-
rigines of Sarawak. From certain superstitions
regarding food," went on Mr. Skelton, " it is
conjectured that their religion was Hinduism.
They will not eat deer, beef or butter, and they
never drink milk. They were happy, peaceful
and contented in their villages until their country
became perpetually attacked by piratical Malay
hordes sent on predatory expeditions against
them by the Sultan of Brunei and his Malayan
princes. The great White Rajah fought for
them and protected them, and they worship his
memory."

I felt I was getting on quite nicely, and thoroughly enjoyed my lesson. " Wait a bit," I said. " Land-Dyaks—Hindu extraction—peaceful—not head-hunters. Well, go on ! Where are the head-hunters and people like Lintong established in Sarawak ? " " Now it becomes more complicated," said my friend. " Sarawak is a country populated by many tribes, different in race and whence blown on to Borneo remains a mystery to this day. Shall I tell you about cranium formation ? " " For Heaven's sake, don't ! " I said. " Quite beyond me. I don't much care about taking notes on people's brain-pans." (Can it be that I imagined a wave of pity passing over Mr. Skelton's face !) " Well," he said, " this much you *would* like to know," and he pointed to the interior of the country. " In the northern portion of the Rejang river were tribes called Kayans, and they had here and there congregated amidst the mountains and along the streams. No one could tell how long these people had inhabited Borneo. They were warlike and head-hunters and tattooed. They were found in some numbers towards the north-east and north-west of Borneo and a good many tribes live in Sarawak territory and are subjects of the Rajah."

Mr. Skelton then told me that many of the Sea-Dyaks—inveterate head-hunters—had migrated to the Rejang, Lintong being one of them. These people were apparently partly Malayan, who, advancing from the south-west portion of

Borneo, had migrated in numbers to the Rejang
and Batang Lupar rivers, from which they drove
the Kayans before them into the interior of the
country. Finally, my friend swept his finger up
the coast-line of Sarawak. " And here, within
fifty miles of the interior, we find the Malayas
established along the coast. They are supposed
to have come from a place called Menangkabo,
in Sumatra. At one time, before the West interfered in Borneo, they ruled over the whole island.
They have a much higher civilization than any
of the savage tribes. Some of them can read
and write, and they make use of Arabic characters for their very limited Malayan literature.
They read the Khoran in Arabic, or pretend to,
as they are Mohammedans, but, excepting those
who have gone Hadji-ing to Mecca, do not
understand one word."

At this point the Rajah returned from Court,
and as we stood to receive him, I said, " Mr.
Skelton has been telling me a lot about Sarawak
—all so interesting." A friendly smile at his
officer, as my husband went on his way to bathe
and dress. " Oh, I daresay," he vouchsafed, as
he walked away. " Skelton always talks too
much." " So like him," said Skelton admiringly,
to me ! And we parted to dress for breakfast.

.   .   .   .   .

The Rajah had returned to Kuching for a
day or two in order to take me back with him
to Sibu, where his presence would, in the course

of a week or so, restore a complete sense of security to the Malays, Chinese and others living there. The attack on the Fort had aroused a certain amount of unrest among tribes here and there scattered further up the river and inland.

Experienced as he was in the behaviour of his manifold subjects, the Rajah thought it necessary to take precautions for our safety. To this end the " Heartsease " was provided with a network of wire stretching round the vessel from the awning to the taffrail, so that any sudden attack upon the ship would be frustrated. Accordingly, early one morning, the Rajah, Mr. Skelton, myself and Ima went on board, where, inside the netting, I felt as though I were a bird in a cage. How lovely ! I thought, feeling important and like heroines " about to face danger with a smile on my lips," but, as it behoves me to write and tell no lies, I did not much believe in the danger, although I thoroughly enjoyed the precautions being taken.

I delighted in the journey. The sea was smooth outside the bar, the flying-fish fascinated me, and the curious effect of the Nipa forests which lined the coasts on the horizon, appearing to stand in mid-air, astonished and interested me. I have heard it said since, and have also read in accounts of that part of the world, that those mirage effects are very strange and wonderful. The Rajah did not respond to my inquiries about it. Neither did Mr. Skelton. They failed to see any reason for my excitement on the subject. But of course they had more important matters to talk about.

We anchored that night in the broad, smooth waters of the Rejang, and arrived at Sibu early the next morning. A salute of twenty-one guns was fired from the Fort to acquaint the inhabitants with their Rajah's return, and on going ashore we were welcomed by a goodly company of Malays, Dyaks and Chinese.

Sibu Fort, surrounded by a grassy lawn, appeared as though standing in an expanse of water. The river at high tide is level with the top of the bank, and so broad at that point that the opposite shore is hardly visible. The Rejang is one of the most important rivers in the country and is navigable, even for a good-sized ship, for over a hundred miles.

I remember how, late in the afternoon of our arrival, the Rajah, Mr. Skelton and I went for a walk through the Sibu bazaar, where the Chinese had built for themselves a row of shops. As everyone knows, the Chinese are the tradesmen of the East and they are to be found all over Malaya, wherever two or three are gathered together. Judging from the flourishing trade of Sibu, they must find shopkeeping a lucrative business. As we were walking past one of the larger shops in the bazaar, I noticed an aged Chinaman under the awning, sitting on a wonderfully inlaid and glazed red-and-black case shaped like a coffin. It turned out to be a real coffin, which he had made for himself in case he should die in Sibu, in order that his corpse might be shipped off—coffin prepaid—to find a burial in his own country, for Chinamen, although they wander all over the globe, are averse to their bones being put away in an alien land. Very poetic, I thought, and yet I failed to grasp the idea of pleasure being derived from sitting smoking an opium pipe on one's own coffin whilst watching the sunset outside one's front door. I remember that walk so well, for, in addition to the coffin incident, we were escorted by a quartet of Sibu fort-men with loaded muskets, as there were rumours of discontented up-river Dyaks about, wriggling in and out of shrubs and the high grass in the neighbourhood of the Fort, ready for a dig at the Rajah and those who accompanied him in his daily necessary walks. Loaded muskets—ourselves walking inside the defending party. Again I felt like a heroine—but again nothing happened.

After three or four days at Sibu, the Rajah sailed in the " Heartsease " for Kapit, near the vanquished rebels' country up the river, and I was left in the care of Mr. Skelton.

A few days after my husband's departure, in the middle of the night, Ima (who slept in my room) and I were hurtled out of our sleep by the sound of a rifle being fired in the Court Room next door. Then thumps on the wall and Mr.

Skelton's voice calling out that the Fort might be attacked, and he must post fort-men in my room to watch that corner of the Fort. I always slept in a sarong, and, quickly putting on a jacket, Ima and I came out of the room. I found the whole place astir, and a very perturbed Mr. Skelton, with three of his men, loading the cannons which poked their noses out of the portholes in the ironwood walls, and placing fort-men with loaded muskets on guard at the lattice-work between roof and walls that encircled the building. Mr. Skelton said, " We are really quite safe here but I hope you are not frightened." " Frightened ! " said I, with a lofty smile, " of course not ! " Frightened or no, I nevertheless took Ima and myself off to sit on the floor of the room behind a small cottage piano I had brought with me from Kuching, as I imagined with good reason that behind such a rampart any spear thrown by the enemy and finding its way through the lattice-work could not reach us. Poor Mr. Skelton ! My presence must have been an awful worry to him. From time to time he kept on pushing at me (sitting behind the piano) plates containing slices of cold ham, which I had to refuse, as I did not like ham and did not feel hungry. At length the dark hours wore themselves away. At dawn the most strenuous precautions were taken, that being the hour always chosen by the Dyaks for their attacks. But nothing happened, and when the sun shone forth we saw that the river ran its way undisturbed by canoes of any description, the grass-plots round the Fort were quite deserted and no human being was to be seen anywhere outside. Ima and I, stiff from our long crouchings on the floor, crept back to my room to lie down and sleep, but before we went to sleep Ima said to me, " Rajah Ranee, she know why Tuan Resident give her ham ? " " No," I said, " Ima, I don't." " Because," said Ima, " Tuan Resident think ham prevent Rajah Ranee get baby if Rajah Ranee frightened." I know that according to mid-Victorian standards I should, at this point, have blushed and looked down, instead of which I am sorry to say that I was intensely amused and laughed heartily. " Oh dear ! " I said to myself, " poor Mr. Skelton ! No doubt he felt nervous, as he knows all about it."

Mr. Skelton and his fort-men, having so recently experienced Lintong's attempted surprise attack, had evidently become somewhat apprehensive, but what really happened was this. A very serious fresh up-river, occasioned by torrents of rain, had been the means of loosening enormous trees from the banks, and these trees, floated by the incoming tide and then swept down by the current, had appeared in the night to the fort-men on the look-out like a number of war boats drifting past the Fort. Thus the disturbance began—and ended in nothing !

When the Rajah returned a few days later he

was much put out on hearing of the occurrence. Mr. Skelton, he said, should have known better than to imagine another attack practicable when he, himself, was patrolling the upper waters of the Rejang. However, kind as he was to all his officials, my husband's displeasure did not last long, as he thought my presence in the Fort at such a time might have made Mr. Skelton nervous and extra apprehensive.

Before closing this chapter I might give a short account of the Rajah's dealing with this refractory tribe. One example will suffice. As already stated, the Rajah had left Sibu for Kapit, as that Fort lay in the neighbourhood of the ci-devant rebels' village and stronghold. As we also knew, the tribe were now homeless, wandering hither and thither, living in their war canoes as and where best they could. The Rajah sent out emissaries in all directions to summon them to a meeting at Kapit Fort. A large number of the tribe appeared, as appointed, to meet my husband, who was surrounded by his loyal chiefs and certain of his Dyak followers. One of the Rajah's officials wrote down in English an account of the proceedings which he had prepared for our monthly magazine, the *Sarawak Gazette*. This is what occurred. " The Rajah, having taken his position in the large Court Room of the Fort, surrounded by his Dyak allies who had been the means of conquering the rebels, the vanquished tribesmen were commanded to appear.

They looked shy and downcast as they entered the guard-room. The Rajah sat himself down on the floor, signing to all present to do likewise, when, after so doing, the vanquished ones appeared to be more at their ease. Then the Rajah addressed them :—' I am glad to find you all here ' (of course he talked to them in the Dyak language) ' meeting you face to face, a sign you bear no malice and that you realize you brought your punishment on yourselves. You must remember how often I have told you not to attack your neighbours or to kill innocent persons. But my words had no effect, and you imagined that my Government forces had no power to reach your mountain stronghold. Now, my friends here, these two great chiefs whom I have known for forty years, would never be guilty of murderous attacks. Yet, remember, I have not come here to kill you, but to become your friend. You have experienced the inconvenience of being attacked and burned out of house and home. I regret the necessity for such action and trust that it may not have to occur again. In future I hope your chiefs will spend their time in keeping their young generation in order.' The vanquished ones then gave tongue. The spokesman, a Dyak from their party, acknowledged they had brought their punishment on themselves and that the Rajah's lesson was none too severe, and his words ended the séance.''

After this a feeling of good-fellowship prevailed, they all shook hands with each other, the Rajah himself joining in, and the chiefs and their tribesmen went their way most cheerfully in the best of tempers.

So there it all was. What children they were, those darling Dyaks! So amenable to kindness though so undisciplined and turbulent in their way. Truly, the Rajah had a large and scattered nursery to keep in order all over his country of Sarawak.

CHAPTER IX

AFTER staying a week or so longer at Sibu, the Rajah was anxious to take me on a visit to Simang-gang, on the Batang Lupar river, the scene of many of his exploits against former head-hunting tribes, and where, with needed severity, kindness and his personal influence the rebels had been brought to understand that a peaceful and useful life was, after all, a better state of things than surreptitious murder.

We therefore, as usual, set out at cockcrow, steaming from Sibu down the broad and uninteresting Igan river, when, after sighting two small green islands at the mouth, we spent a few hours at sea which—as it was very rough—sent me to my cabin. We then entered the Batang Lupar river, very broad at the mouth and uninteresting, with its low shores and never-ending Nipa forests. I was then, and am now, very ignorant of geology and the vagaries of earth formation, but from what I learned then I imagine that nowhere in the world does the land so encroach upon the sea. For instance, if you look at a map of Sarawak, you will notice that from the mouth of the river that flows through Kuching the land near the coast, with the exception of some hills—call them mountains if you like, they are about 1000 feet high—forms a vast plain until the river Oyah is reached. This is caused by the vast amount of rain which, falling on the mountains in the interior, forces the hundreds of tiny springs to swell and rush down to the sea, carrying with them in their headlong course great quantities of earth. On nearing the sea, this muddy earth attracts those mud-loving trees called Nipas, which seed themselves as they proceed and, encroaching with their black spidery roots, take possession of the shore. If you examine them at low tide the myriads of roots look like closely woven netting from which spring great crowns of branches with tiny leaves, and at the end of each branch hangs a long tassel-shaped crimson fruit. For ever at work, the trees drop their fruit into the mud, and so, unceasingly, more and more, the Nipa forests encroach upon the sea. One old Malay was known to say that during his life the land had thus extended itself for more than a mile.

Captain Helyar, who commanded the " Hearts-ease," told me about the Nipas when I went on the bridge as we entered the smooth water of the river. We anchored for the night abreast Lingga Fort, where the Rajah had spent ten years of his life alone, without English companionship, leading numberless expeditions, backed by devoted Dyak followers, against head-hunters. Hardly ever at rest by day or night, he managed to bring peace and security to the whole district, till at length the most hardened miscreants flocked around his banner and became decent law-abiding men.

And Lingga—only picture a square wooden fort built on a mud-bank, replete with discomfort inside. Ten of the best years of his life spent in such a place, with no reward of any kind to be hoped for beyond the knowledge that his heroic life was advancing the betterment of the people. At the time of our visit the Fort had been practically abandoned. The river was at peace, and there stood Lingga Fort in its old age, its work done, and, like all old things—human and otherwise—forgotten by most, notwithstanding the storms that once raged around it.

Although the Batang Lupar river is dangerous for any vessel bigger than a good-sized war-boat or canoe, the Rajah was averse from letting me travel for so many miles in a river boat, thinking it would be too tiring for me; so he decided to steam thither in the "Heartsease." Good gracious! What a journey! Captain Helyar was pale with apprehension. Owing to a bore, that part of the river could never be accurately charted. At new and full moon, owing to the action of the tides, the channel was necessarily altered. "Never mind," said my husband cheerily, "in for a penny, in for a pound!" and he thoroughly enjoyed himself. As a matter of fact, we stuck on several sandbanks, which the

yacht evidently disliked. Free from one sand-
bank we ran on to another, and took the whole
day to reach Simanggang Fort. I did wonder
whether or no, here and there, we might be in
danger of annihilation ! But, knowing nothing
of navigation, I did not worry much. " Where
ignorance is bliss ! " . . .

When first I visited Simanggang Fort there
was, for the time being, no English Resident in
charge. On our arrival we were met by a crowd
of Malays and Dyaks who awaited us at the
Fort's landing-place. Three prominent Malays,
who were the officers in charge of the Residency,
received us. For years they had been devoted
to the Rajah, who appreciated their rectitude,
their devotion and the manner in which they
had so ably helped in the civilization of Sarawak.
Pangeran Matali, one of the three, had been
originally a prince at the Sultan of Brunei's
Court. Abang Aing belonged to the most
respected family in Simanggang and Tonko
Mohammed had been on a pilgrimage to Mecca.
Courtly in manner, like my dear Datus in
Kuching, they helped the Rajah and myself
out of the yacht's dinghy. They were delighted
to see their beloved Rajah and appeared to be
ready to bestow their affection on me. The
rest of the Malays and Dyaks came forward as
we stepped on shore so that each one in turn
might touch our fingers. This custom had been
instituted by the first Rajah Brooke, who insisted

(and very rightly) that no subject of his should grovel on the ground, Eastern fashion, before his ruler.   The somewhat lengthy ceremony over, my husband led the way up the ensennah-bordered avenue to the Fort, I following with the three Malay officials in attendance. We parted at the entrance to the Fort, when my husband let it be known that he would hold a reception of all his subjects in the evening after dinner.   Accordingly, after we had partaken of our roast chicken, prawn curry and custard apples (we took our Chinese cook from Kuching with us on our expeditions), we were ready for the party to begin.   The large room was cleared and places arranged for ourselves and the three grave and reverend signors at one end of the hall.   The rest of the company sat on the floor, leaving a space in the centre for the Dyak dances with which we were to be specially entertained later.   The Rajah looked so happy, surrounded by his three old friends, all four puffing at their Manila cheroots.   I was interested in the way the three officials held their cheroots in the cleft of the thumb and forefinger, the palm of the hand showing outwards.   Later in life, when I took to cigarettes, I tried to imitate this fashion, but without success.   I sat there contentedly watching our subjects seated on the floor.   They none of them talked to one another, but now and again the silence would be broken by the sound of severe scratching, signifying that mos-

quitoes were at work on somebody's flesh, while
every little while a sudden smack sounded the
death-knell of one of those tiresome insects.
The Dyak orchestra then made its appearance—
six or seven young warriors in chawats (loin-
cloths) much be-bangled on legs and arms.
Very serious they looked as they sat themselves
down around the cleared space in the centre,
and forthwith began to rattle and bang and
thump gongs and drums, large and small, with
perfect rhythm and almost unbearable noise.
After a few minutes of such overture, a Dyak in
full war costume, bear-skin jacket, a head-hand-
kerchief, over which waved a hornbill plume—
denoting that he had taken heads in warfare—
bounded into the room, waving an object which
at first I took to be a coco-nut. He leaped high
and capered about, but was so light of foot that
he made no noise on the floor. As he came near
us in the dance, I saw that what I had taken to
be a coco-nut was a human skull! I felt quite
sick at the sight, and rushed out of the hall to
the bedroom next door, which I reached just in
time to act as bad sailors are wont to do at sea,
after which I flopped on to the floor. Hearing
the noise of my fall, the Rajah came to see what
had happened and quickly pulled me up into a
sitting position. "What is the matter, Margaret?" he inquired in quite an ordinary tone,
while I sat looking at him and blinking sillily.
"Surely you are not frightened?" "Oh," I

said, " you see, Charlie, I have never seen skulls brought out at parties before!" "What an idea!" he replied; "the head-dance is one of the most important dances among Dyaks. It was a special entertainment got up in our honour! Can't you come back again?" I was sorry for the people's disappointment but *did* feel a bit off-colour. "No, Charlie," I said, "I really don't feel that I can. I must go to bed." The poor dear looked rather cast down. A bright thought came to me. "Do tell them from me that I don't feel well—that I am going to have a baby, and that made me go away." He evidently approved, departed, and through the Malay officials my message was given to the people. The dances were resumed and the Rajah and his guests sat smoking and watching them far into the night. . . .

A morning or two later we left Simanggang, and the " Heartsease " having once again waltzed and hesitated its way back through the uncharted waters of the Batang Lupar river, we anchored opposite a Dyak house (or village) that stood on a high bank overlooking the stream. This house was divided into compartments, or rooms, and sheltered some 250 souls under its low palm-thatched roof. Each family enjoyed a privacy all its own, and the house contained in addition two very large reception rooms situated in the centre, one for the men and one for the women, where they could all meet together or receive visitors from outside. Like all Dyak houses, it was built on poles of timber and bamboo some thirty feet high, and in order to get inside it was necessary to climb up a pole from which notches had been hacked out so that it served as a stairway. After we landed we were conducted to this house, and I then realized what was before me. Nothing for it—we each and all of us had to climb the pole! The Rajah, accustomed to such primitive staircases, hopped lightly and easily up. I looked at it with a somewhat uneasy feeling, but up I had to go. Abang Aing took charge, and chose two hefty young Dyaks from out of the crowd to lead my faltering footsteps. " Turn out your feet, Rajah Ranee, and you will find it quite easy," said Abang Aing. With one young Dyak holding on to my right arm and thus leading me in front, and t'other Dyak holding on to my left hand, I turned my feet out to the fifth position in dancing lessons at every notch, and somehow found myself at last, without mishap, on the long gallery that ran outside the rooms. " Thank God that's over! " I thought to myself, but felt sad that my entrance as Ranee had been so devoid of dignity and grace. At once I was surrounded by the women, who took possession of me and clung to me in a most affectionate manner, leading me into their own large reception room, while the Rajah was escorted to the men's quarters. Again I felt happy to be among the women—my kind friends—whom I loved and admired, with their glowing eyes, shining black hair, delicate limbs and sleek gleaming bodies so exquisitely clean—like all Sarawak people they almost live in the water. Their thick cotton petticoats, woven by themselves, were brown and tan in colour and their waistbands were made of rattans in dark red and brown shades, while they wore many bangles of silver and brass.

I was led up to a raised seat in the middle of the room. This had been covered with some yellow cloth which was the only bright note of colour, all the rest was brown or tan—the walls were brown, the ceilings, the women's clothes, only their faces were a pale yellow as they sat on a large mat covering the floor. They smiled at me and looked so kind. They talked to me, but I could not understand a word they said. The Chief's wife and some others stroked and patted me gently, making crooning noises such as one would to a baby. " Oom—oom—oom," they crooned, and pushed up my sleeve, a very loose one, far above my elbow, after which they pointed to their own arms, shook their heads and smiled, meaning they had found out that I was white all over. We were getting along very well, feeling that, whether white or brown, we all belonged to one big family, and I was enjoying my new experience, when an ominous creaking noise was heard. The floor was giving way underneath us. Being unable to bear the weight of the unusually large numbers surrounding me in the hall, the bamboos and light supporting timbers cracked and bent, unequal to the strain, and I found myself, seat and all, together with some ten or twelve of my entourage, sinking into an abyss. All the women began to scream " Rajah Ranee gone under the house !! " An awful row was going on. The Rajah, in the next room, with great presence of mind, remained where he was, for fear of a panic, but sent two or three of his trusty followers to our aid. They ordered all the women who could do so to leave the hall, and then they set to work to help me, the Chief's wife and the rest of the engulfed women from our dangerous plight. I don't think we could have gone down more than ten feet or so, the mat having behaved admirably on the occasion, but, oh dear ! the process of extricating our bodies, fallen helter-skelter down the hole, was a lengthy and complicated one. The Dyak women, small, slight and agile, were comparatively easy to pull out, but I was more difficult to deal with. When at last I found myself once more on firm ground, safe and unhurt, I could not help thinking what an escape I had had. But whatever happened, accidents or no, I felt when I said good-bye to them that I had left a bit of my heart behind with the Dyak women of the Batang Lupar river. We embarked in the " Heartsease " and steamed back to Kuching, where we arrived late next day.

Some time was to elapse before I could indulge in more wanderings up and down the country, for a week later my baby was born at the Astana. It was a girl, and the Rajah, although disappointed, was very kind about it. Although I loved my baby dearly I thought this latest experience a most unpleasant one, superintended as it was by our rather unsympathetic doctor and a Malay " Mrs. Gamp."

CHAPTER X

Notwithstanding my harum-scarum flittings, my journeys over the country in my expectant condition and the pessimistic warnings of Mrs. Helms regarding the dangers to my health of such proceedings, my infant and myself progressed quite satisfactorily. The Rajah, quite easy in his mind concerning my flourishing state of health, took himself off for a cruise to one or two Residencies on the coast the day after the baby's arrival, and I was left for the time being in the care of our doctor and my Malay nurse. The first day or two passed quietly, when excitement began regarding the baby's food. Owing to personal disqualifications which I could not control, it became necessary to resort to artificial nourishment for the infant. The absence of cows in Kuching was a difficulty. Preserved milk was tried, but the baby's inside resented it. Excitement and anxiety weighed heavily on the doctor and the nurse. Datu Isa, informed by Talip of the difficulty, rushed up to the Astana. " Kambing," [1] she cried, " dapat susu kambing ! " [2] whereupon messages were sent up and down Kuching to find the required goat;

[1] Goat.　　　　[2] Find goat's milk.

after which my Malay " Gamp," with her head out of the window in expectation of the arrival of " kambing," shouted at me as I lay in my mosquito house, the baby at my side yelling for food, " Here they come—one, two, three—*ten* kambings ! They tie them to the house near the entrance ! " And indeed the owners had left them there, an incongruous-looking group of animals, blocking up our front door. The doctor examined them and chose the healthiest from out the lot, whereupon the nine disappointed " kambing " owners were sent for to lead their unwanted animals back to their homes. The doctor highly approved of Datu Isa's suggestion, the experiment proved successful, the baby thrived on the goat's-milk régime, and after the intense excitement all went well in my newly-inaugurated nursery. Datu Isa, delighted with the result of her brain-wave, was a constant visitor in my room. She seemed to feel that she was responsible for me. What a darling she was ! she and those other beloved Malay women who were constantly at my side during my convalescence. They were the greatest joy and comfort to me in my somewhat solitary life and their devotion and kindness certainly helped me to make a speedy recovery.

Meanwhile, during the last few months, three or four more English ladies had come out to Kuching from England. The Bishop's chaplain and his wife, Mr. and Mrs. Kemp, had been bidden thither in order to reinforce the pastoral staff. Mrs. Kemp was young, charming, most kind and a great asset to our English society. Mrs. Chambers' niece, too, came out to join her aunt and very soon one of the Rajah's officials was attracted by her and the young people married and lived happily ever after. One or two others also joined the groups, newly appointed officials and their wives. One of those sirens happened to be a pianist, and when, presently, I was able to resume our weekly dinner-parties, an addition was made to the musical programme by the lady who, of her own accord, seated herself at the piano and gave us that early-Victorian *morceau* " La prière d'une Vierge! " This chaste melody with its sweet and unexciting simplicity roused in the breasts of all present visions of homely, and almost stuffy, propriety.

The English ladies were always kind to me. Mrs. Kemp loved my baby, and when, later, children were born to her in Kuching, we were naturally much drawn together in our interest in one another's infants. And yet I was always amazed and disappointed at the lack of interest they showed in the country which was—at any rate for the time being—their home. I used to wonder why white people should be so conceited and imagine themselves to be so inordinately superior to those whom they chose to class together as " blacks! " After all, the East has been the foundation of all that is best in Europe.

My dear Malay friends might, every one of them, have taught many a lesson of devotion, of gratitude, of usefulness in family life, in weaving beautiful designs and embroidering exquisite patterns in gold and silver. It is only by making *real* friends with these people and getting to know them well that one can appreciate the simple, useful orderliness of their home lives. In those days English people simply wallowed in reminiscences of England, recalling almost morbidly how Mrs. Smith of Croydon invariably managed to produce a dish of asparagus from her garden at Easter, and so on. . . . But I must say that never did I hear any depreciatory remarks made about our subjects by any of the officers on the Rajah's staff. So their wives might cackle as they pleased, their words carried no weight and were only of interest to themselves.

I lived in two different worlds—the world of my stilted conventional English friends and the world of my warm-hearted Malay women who, although they were encouraged by me to come and go freely in the Astana, never at any time forgot the respect due to me as their Rajah's wife. They possessed that natural tact and discretion that masters the heart when one truly loves. Friendship is a most gentle thing, and they respected our friendship and handled it with delicacy. Perfectly secure in our mutual attitude, we managed to have great fun. In and out of my rooms would these dear women go.

In my bedroom my cheval glass was a great delight to them. They had never before seen such a thing. They would smile and curtsey to themselves, turning away from their reflections and looking back over their shoulders, preening themselves and strutting like little peacocks in the sun. On fine evenings we would walk about the garden on the well-kept lawns where, among the roses, gardenias and other sweet-smelling flowers, the south wind from the sea blew freshness into our faces, mingled with the scent of far-off blossoms, blooming unseen in the heart of the great woods.

Although, at that time, the women of Kuching could neither read nor write, in most towns and villages in Sarawak there are to be found ancient dames who have somehow come to live among the Sarawak Malays—maybe from Singapore or other Malayan countries—who have learned in some way to read the Arabic character. My friends could tell me nothing about those women except that they were paid small sums occasionally to come and read to them legends of zman dulu (olden times). The legends most pleasing to their audience were those relating to the lives of the Sultans, Rajahs, Queens and Princesses of earlier days. This gave me the idea that it would be an additional interest in their lives if they could read and write in their own language. When I asked them about it, several of the younger married women were eager to begin, particularly

Daiang Sahada, Datu Isa's daughter-in-law. So
I sent for Inchi Sawal, then living in Kuching,
who was versed in Malay lore and taught the
Rajah's officials how to write the language when
they came out to join his staff. As Malay women
are not supposed to meet with men other than
their husbands or near relations, I arranged that
Inchi Sawal should teach me and that I should
pass on his teachings to my friends. He came
once a week and instructed me in the writing of
the Arabic alphabet (lovely characters, but oh,
so difficult to write properly !). However, I got
on somehow and after the lesson some six or
seven of my Malay friends would come to the
Astana, eager to delve in my brain for the few
seeds of Arabic script that Inchi Sawal had
planted therein. With our tongues out, so ab-
sorbed were we in our efforts at advancement,
we would cover sheets and sheets of paper with
rather wobbly and not very satisfactory characters. All except Daiang Sahada, who outran
us all very rapidly, and in an amazingly short
time managed to write out in Malay verse of
her own composition the story of Sarawak from
the first days of the second Rajah Brooke.

I am sorry to say that our dear Datu Isa did
not share in our enthusiasm for education. She
came to see me on the subject. " Oh, Rajah
Ranee," she said, as she pounded together betel
and coco-nut in preparation for subsequent chewing, " for our women to know how to write is a

dangerous precedent. The virgins will be writing
love-letters to their swains, and throwing them
into their canoes as they drift by under their
windows. Dangerous, very dangerous indeed ! "
I listened with the greatest attention to the old
lady's admonishments and much quieted her by
promising that I would ask the Rajah's opinion
on the matter. Needless to say my husband
knew of, and rather approved, my endeavours
to instil a desire for education into his women
subjects. When I told him of Datu Isa's mis-
givings he just smiled and said, " Go on with
what you are doing and tell Datu Isa from me
she need have no fear of the young women of
Kuching throwing letters about broadcast. They
have too much reverence for her ever to do anything of which she would not approve." I
thought that my husband's handling of so thorny
a subject could not have been bettered. I gave
Datu Isa her Rajah's message, over which she
purred with delight and found no more fault
with the writings, which went on as before.
Truly, tact is able to do great things, but how
few there are who possess the golden gift !

At this time the Rajah was for ever going off
on trips of supervision up and down the country,
and now that the incubus of infant production
was over for the time I delighted in happy hours
spent with my Malay friends in the garden of
the Astana. We had so many interests to share.
The newly-made mothers among them would

bring their babies to compare with mine and we would compliment each other on the beauty of one another's child products. What lovely little things those Malay infants were, with their skins of pale apricot! When I used to say this to their mothers they would look at my baby and say, " Rajah Ranee have much prettier baby with skin like milk."

We were all soon enjoying our parties again, walking about the garden, drinking tea and eating cakes under the trees. The presence of two beautiful peacocks proved a source of interest and delight to my guests. " So like zman dulu," they used to say, for in olden times Ranees and Princesses were always surrounded in their gardens by peacocks and other lovely birds. Great games they had with them too! The virgins (daiang daiangs) in their beautiful silken robes and tinkling ornaments would, by their antics, induce the birds to follow them. They used to drag bits of string baited with fruit along the ground, gently teasing them, whereupon the peacocks would pursue them, flutter about, and try to peck the girls' feet. This caused them the greatest amusement, but the peacocks rarely succeeded, as the maidens were too quick and agile for them. Once, however, the peacocks, foiled in their attempts to peck the girls' feet, made a deliberate onslaught on the toes of the Dyak fort-man who, in forage cap and white drill uniform, was doing sentry duty at one of the doors of the Astana near by. His surprise was so great, the bird having drawn blood, that the poor man threw down his musket and rushed off to the other side of the building, the peacock in hot pursuit. One of the gardeners, seeing what had happened, drove off the bird, the sentry then returned to his post and all was well. Datu Isa and I agreed that nothing should be said to the Rajah and the Datus about the poor sentry's lapse in discipline for fear that an end might be put to the bird frolics. And the peacocks continued to provide unfailing entertainment for my guests.

Those garden parties! How can I ever forget the swift change from day into night, when suddenly from brilliant sunshine the great red disc would disappear behind Mount Matang, while a tiny streak of silver would appear above the horizon, mild and lovely on a rosy bed of mist, to be followed at certain seasons by Venus, the star of love! Often, before parting for the night, we would look over towards the north, to Santubong, the mountain by the sea, whose jagged outline bears a striking resemblance to the profile of the great White Rajah. " See," the women would say to me, " the gods were aware of his advent in Sarawak and drew his picture for ever across the sky." Then my friends would get into their canoes and return to their homes. I would watch the boats receding from my sight, the paddles making a pretty rhythmic sound as they ploughed up the water. Our fun had ended for that day. Night had come. I would then feel very lonely and go back to the Astana, sit on the verandah and watch the stars, my thoughts all muddled in my brain. Was I happy or not? I wondered. I did not know. And there I would sit, and sometimes begin to cry. Then I would shake myself together and go into the nursery to look at my sleeping baby watched over by her Malay nurse.

When the Rajah was away on his river journeys, although I felt very lonely, there was one distinct advantage in his absence as far as I was concerned. I was able to escape the long and formal dinner and to retire early to bed with a book. The Astana possessed a fine library which had been collected by the first Rajah. Unfortunately for me, however, the volumes contained therein were mostly instructive and very highbrow. But the English residents in Kuching had managed to start a little circulating library, and from this I was able to obtain novels by Miss Braddon, Whyte-Melville, Mrs. Henry Wood, Ouida and others. One day I came across a book about France, and as such books were hardly ever to be found in Kuching, I carried it off at once, thinking how lucky I had been to find it. I went early to bed that night, opened the book, began to read and immediately fell under its spell. It was called *The Village on the Cliff*, and was by Anne Thackeray, daughter of the famous author. The story was about a village by the sea in Normandy. The heroine, as well as most of the other characters, was French. Descriptions were given of the home life of the people, their gay, joyous village festivals, their grape and apple harvests when the heroine and her friends would mount on the top of the rosy fruit in the harvest carts and be drawn in triumph back to their village home. The book was so exquisitely written and the simple gaiety of the French people so vividly set forth that it carried me back to my childhood days, and poignant memories of Epinay came over me. I read every word, came to the end, closed the book and pushed it under my pillow, after which I cried my heart out. I cried so much that I made myself quite ill and was still in bed when the Rajah returned late next morning to find me in tears. Poor dear, he could not make out what was the matter but at once suspected malaria and sent for Dr. Houghton. " Quite right," said the doctor. " A sharp attack ! " And he proceeded to prescribe quinine ! Nowadays " nerves " might have been suspected, but neither the doctor nor my poor husband had any idea that my crying fit had been brought on by an attack of home-sickness, the cause of which lay under my pillow. Luckily for me, the rules and regulations of the library were very lax, for Anne Thackeray's beautiful story was never returned, but remains in my possession to this day and it now reposes on the bookshelves of my Cornish home.

However, the Rajah's return (and the quinine!) did me good. He was very kind, showed no impatience with my sobbing fits, and soon I was able to pull myself together and behave more rationally. A day or two later an event happened calculated to turn my interests into a new and unlooked-for channel.

Whilst the Rajah was at Court one of his officials came to tell me that while walking through the Kuching bazaar early that morning he had met a European accompanied by a Malay wife. They had landed from a Chinese junk which had just anchored in the river. The European, not being able to talk English, had explained to the Rajah's officer in Malay that he and his wife had been on their way from Amboyna (in the Dutch East Indies) to Singapore. He had been employed as teacher in a school in Amboyna, but as he and his wife had disliked their surroundings there they had resolved to set out for Singapore, where he hoped to obtain employment.

The sailing boat in which they had taken passage had been wrecked off the Sarawak coast near the entrance to the river, and had been completely lost. He and his wife and one or two of the crew had been picked up by the

Chinese junk in which he had just arrived at Kuching. The man was a Frenchman, and for this reason the Rajah's official had brought him to me. I told him he had done quite right and that I would see the couple at once. When they were ushered in, both the Frenchman and his Malay wife were rigged out in some rather oddly assorted Chinese clothes which had been given them by a kindly Chinaman on board the junk. The man was about forty-five, of medium height, with dark unkempt hair, whiskers and beard ; his brown eyes had a twinkle in them and he looked intelligent. In spite of his rather grotesque costume a certain air of dignity hung about him and impressed me in his favour. When I spoke to him in French he was obviously delighted. " This gentleman has told me about your misfortunes," I said. " What is your name ? " " Poncelet, Altesse," he said. " My house in France was destroyed at Sédan during the war." " Poncelet and Sédan," I thought ; " how delightfully French ! Now what can I do to help him ? " His accent was perfect. He was evidently an educated man. We must somehow keep him in Kuching—then I should be able to talk French now and then. At this point the Rajah returned from Court and came into my room, whereupon I presented the Frenchman to him, relating at the same time his devastating experiences of shipwreck and losses. The Rajah, who was always kind to those in misery, gave

orders for a suit of his own clothes to be given to
the unfortunate man and told his officer to give
him some money and engage rooms in the
bazaar for the couple until such time as he could
see what could be done for them. The poor
man went off, full of gratitude, in the care of the
official, and my husband and I went to breakfast.
Full of sympathy and plans to help my new
acquaintance, and not being very tactful, I am
afraid I made myself something of a nuisance.
"Oh, Charlie," I said, "do let him give you
French lessons two or three times a week—he
speaks such perfect French! And another thing!
He told me that he loves music and knows something about playing the harmonium. How about
the little organ just given to the church by the
old lady in England? No one can play it.
Couldn't Monsieur Poncelet be appointed organist?" "How you do run on!" said my poor
husband, and relapsed into silence.

However, though he said nothing of his intentions to me, he eventually established Monsieur
Poncelet and his Malay wife in a small bungalow
in Kuching where they lived comfortably till
their death many years later. He also took
French lessons from him three times weekly.
In addition, he induced the Bishop to appoint
him organist in the church. Luckily for all
concerned, neither clergy nor congregation were
at all critical in the matter of music, and listened
on Sundays and Feast Days, quite unmoved, to

the raucous voices of the Chinese choir-boys doing their best to drown the noises produced by the " organist's " undisciplined fingers on the keys of the organ.

Monsieur Poncelet became quite a personage in Kuching. In spite of his somewhat eccentric playing he was genuinely fond of music and confided to me how much he loved Bellini's opera " Lucia." When he spoke the name of the heroine his voice would become quite wobbly. " Que voulez-vous," he used to say, " quand on est jeune on devient amoureux! " I put two and two together and imagined—rightly or wrongly—that there may have been in his youthful days a Lucia embedded in his heart! That, of course, was no business of mine, but, realizing his fondness for the opera, I offered to play it to him. He listened with the greatest satisfaction. So much so that my " Lucia " performances on the piano became weekly ones for his benefit. During the sentimental love passages the tears would come into his eyes, whereupon attention to his nose became necessary. At such moments he would rise from his chair and wave a warning hand at me to ensure silence for a moment. " Attendez, Altesse," he would say, " je vais me moucher." I would wait until the nose was attended to, after which I resumed work ! When the séance was over, the last chord struck, sandwiches, cake and lemonade were brought in for his refreshment. Thus restored, he would go his way with many grateful expressions for the music.

Some months later my brother, Harry de Windt, came out to Sarawak. My husband, having a great affection for him and knowing what pleasure his presence would give me, appointed him his private secretary, which appointment Harry received with gratitude and delight. At the same time Mr. Frank Maxwell, a young man of my own age, joined the Rajah's staff. His devotion to Sarawak and its Rajah can never fade from my mind. We became great friends.

As is well known, the entire island of Borneo belonged at one time to the Dutch, with the exception of the north-western strip lying along the coast for some 500 miles, which was the Rajah's territory, Sarawak, and a portion at the extreme northern point which was then owned by the Sultan of Brunei. The Dutch Government were inclined to look upon us as interlopers on account of the romantic methods of the first Rajah; but as he had been whole-heartedly elected their ruler by the Sarawak people and had secured the protection of the British Government for the country, the Dutch had no choice but to become reconciled to the Rajah's supremacy in Sarawak.

Now it so happened that a state of almost perpetual friction existed between the Dutch and the Sarawak peoples on the frontier, who, true to tradition, were in the habit of carrying away each other's heads. This state of affairs naturally gave rise to recriminations between their respective governments, and on one particular occasion the Dutch Resident in charge of the colony became somewhat disagreeable. Masses of correspondence passed between Sarawak and Dutch Borneo, and finally the Resident of Dutch Borneo wrote a courtly and charming letter to the Rajah, suggesting that he and his wife should pay him a friendly visit at Pontianak, when difficult topics could be discussed. My husband accepted the invitation and we set forth in the " Heartsease," my brother Harry as his secretary and Mr. Skelton as his aide-de-camp. Arrived at Pontianak we found the ships in the harbour all beflagged and dressed for the occasion. A crowd of officials and one Dutch lady were awaiting us on the wharf and gave us a cordial reception. Pontianak was like many of our own stations. The Residency was a spacious bungalow and our quarters were very comfortable and cool. The Rajah and the Resident soon arrived at an amicable settlement of frontier disputes and all went well. The Resident was unmarried and the Dutch lady acted as our hostess. She proved to be talkative and became very confidential. When I expressed surprise at her being the only lady in a colony which harboured so many gentlemen of marriageable age, she promptly confessed that almost all the gentlemen *were* married, but that

their wives had proved so tiresome, each claiming
it as her right and privilege to take me about,
that the Resident had ordered them all to stay
at home and had deputed herself, married to the
youngest and least exalted of his officers, to do
the honours.

Our visit was quite successful. In those days
neither the Rajah (who subsequently became a
fair French scholar) nor Mr. Skelton could talk
French, so they conversed in Malay with the
Dutch gentlemen, who could talk no English,
while my brother and myself talked French better
than English and got on very well. Banquets
were given in our honour and everything was
done to amuse us. For our special entertainment we were taken for an expedition through a
canal which the Resident had but lately cut
through the country from Pontianak to the sea,
where, on our arrival at the coast, we were to
board a gunboat and return up river to Pontianak
for the night. Oh dear, that canal! A mere
ditch in size, down which we paddled and paddled
and paddled. Would the end never come? I
thought. It was impossible to see anything of
the country through which we passed, as the low
awnings of the canoe shut out every object.
The Dutch lady was in the canoe with me;
also the Commandant of the ship awaiting us on
the coast. When at length we arrived at our
destination we found the sea very rough. There
was nothing for it, however, but to embark on

the ship's boat in order to reach the gunboat anchored a mile off. The Rajah, my brother and Mr. Skelton had made their way with the Resident in a different canoe and ship's boat and were already on board waiting for us to join them. The Commandant, assuming a naval deportment, handed me as best he could into the wobbling boat, but had to lift the little Dutch lady in as she was unaccustomed to a seafaring life. Our transit to the ship was not without incident. The waves swept over us and wet us through and through. Although I am invariably sea-sick in steamers, luckily the worst weather has no effect on me in sailing boats or rowing boats. I was therefore able to smile sweetly at the Commandant through it all. But the poor Dutch lady ! She utterly lost command over herself and was fearfully sick, whereupon the Commandant, quite the lady's man, tore her hat off and held her forehead at each paroxysm. When we came abreast the gunboat, the climbing up the steps to the deck with the boat rising and falling with the waves required very drastic measures. Clutching the poor Dutch lady round the middle—much as one would handle a sack of wheat—he managed to throw her into the embrace of a sailor standing by. She was borne to a cabin and seen no more on the trip. " Maintenant, à nous deux," he said, as the boat rose level with the deck one moment and sank down to the lowest gangway step the next. Being accustomed to the exigencies of such situations, I managed to gain the deck without mishap. The Commandant bowed low before me, assumed an attitude and said, " Ah, Altesse, vous êtes une vraie fille d'Albion." I looked round for the same kind of approbation from the Rajah, Mr. Skelton and my brother. None, however, came. " Silly fool! " said my brother. He meant the Commandant.

CHAPTER XI

ON our return to Kuching life went on as usual. Before my little girl had reached her second birthday two baby boys appeared on the scene. Malays have a superstition that twins are unlucky, and in my case the superstition was aggravated by the fact that an eclipse of the sun had taken place in our part of the world two months before they were born. However, my Malay friends were more affectionate than ever and Datu Isa constantly visited us, simply teeming with good advice. My husband, realizing that three babies of that age were more than native nurses and I could cope with, wrote to his relations in England asking them to engage an English nurse to come out and take charge of the children. Superstitious or no, I felt a certain misgiving when the woman arrived, for although her appearance was neat, her features good, her looks were marred by an awful squint. I have always had a feeling that cross-eyed people bring bad luck in a home. But for the time being she was quite satisfactory and managed the fledgelings well.

Feeling that they were in competent hands I was able occasionally to accompany my husband on his journeys up country. We visited Mukah,

situated on the coast. Now Mukah and another
Residency further north, called Bintulu, had been
ceded to Sarawak by the Sultan of Brunei about
ten years previously, thus adding some 110 miles
to the coast-line of Sarawak. This action on the
part of the Sultan had been compulsory, as the
people of those districts had become restless and
dissatisfied under his autocratic, self-seeking and
devastating rule, and had clamoured to become
the subjects of Sarawak's White Rajah and live
under his benevolent government.

Mukah was famous for its sago plantations, for
even in my time our Borneo Company in Sarawak exported great quantities of that well-known
nursery pudding food.

As this was my first trip at sea since the arrival
of my babies I was anxious to do my best to
combat sea-sickness. I had been told that champagne was a panacea for that malady, especially
on short journeys, and knowing that when we
left the mouth of the river we would have an
eight hours' sea passage to Mukah, I determined
to resort to this supposedly infallible remedy.
My first care, therefore, when I went on board
the " Heartsease " was to order a bottle of champagne to be sent down to my cabin. My orders
were carried out, and as the yacht prepared to
bob and curtsey her way across the bar I promptly
went down to my state-room, seized the bottle
and began to drink glass after glass of the wine.
Exhilaration quickly came on and I continued

my potations until the bottle was nearly empty. There I lay, impervious to all things, and began to sing. Although quite ignorant of my behaviour at the time, I was told by the Rajah subsequently that through the panes of the open skylight that separated my cabin from the deck, " A Life on the Ocean Wave," " Tom Bowling," and " Rule Britannia " were squeaked out in a somewhat uncertain soprano. On hearing the nautical strains he presently descended to inquire into my condition, by which time I had fallen into a state of coma. He glanced at the empty bottle at my side, realized what had happened, shut the door of the cabin and went back on deck, leaving me to my slumbers until the anchor was dropped some hours later opposite the Fort of Mukah, when he came to fetch me. Though still slightly muzzy and a trifle incoherent, I managed with his help to get on deck and into the dinghy which took us ashore, where the Resident, Mr. de Crespigny, and the principal ministers and officials were awaiting us. The noise of the Rajah's salute fired from the Fort, the general excitement of his arrival and the subsequent greetings helped to distract attention from me, although luckily the symptoms of my injudicious imbibings were rapidly wearing off. Later, when we were alone before dinner, the Rajah told me about my ill-chosen time for singing songs, remarking quite kindly that it was out of place. I told him what a marvellous preventive of sea-sickness I had found, which amused him intensely. "My dear," he said, "when next you have recourse to champagne as a medicine, be careful how you measure out the doses!" I need hardly say that such behaviour on my part did not occur again.

I found Mukah a very interesting station. I had had no idea that the sago which we all know so well in England as a popular milk pudding was a product of the palm tree. I had always imagined that it was grown like wheat, oats or similar cereals, so limited was the education doled out to children of the mid-Victorian era. Mukah was surrounded by beautiful palm forests growing in all directions by the sea. "But *how* do they produce the sago from the palms?" I inquired. "From pith in their insides," was the answer; and it all seemed wonderful to me. But then, to an inquiring mind, wonders *never* cease. They are part of one's daily life. Take the earthworms under our feet; the pebbles which we kick aside. Whence do they come? Even the great Shakespeare himself, talking through Hamlet, confesses his wonderment about things that are met with every day. It seemed to me that I knew nothing about anything and that I was constantly coming upon fresh marvels. But to return to sago. First of all the beautiful palm, which grows only in salt marshes, has to be cut down, the trunk is split in two and from the heart a creamy, sticky substance is scraped out with a board studded with spikes and dropped on a mat spread on a wooden platform under which a canoe is floating. The method employed is a primitive one. A native worker, the extractor, then pours water over the mass and works it with his feet by dancing a fandango on it. The process is repeated several times and thus a thick liquid is detached and flows through the perforated mat into the empty canoe prepared for its reception. This is added to by other workers, and when the canoe is filled to capacity it is taken to the refinery of the Borneo Company, where it goes through the final process from which it emerges exquisitely pure, ready for shipment to the English market. Both young men and girls work at extracting the product from the palms, but the particularly graceful dance is only performed by the men and is eagerly watched by the Milanoe ladies who congregate in crowds on such occasions, and the happy ballerinos receive many tokens of admiration from female onlookers. A less pleasing feature of the sago production is the horrible smell which the crushed pith emits. I noticed it even on our arrival in the yacht and I am sorry to say that I found Mukah the most evil-smelling spot I have ever known. Oddly enough, too, on returning from a tour round the place in a paddle boat, I noticed that my bangles and the golden ornaments I wore had turned quite black. I inquired the reason of this and was answered with apparent satisfaction, "The sago smell, Rajah Ranee, the sago smell!"

From the Fort, which was situated near the sea, I was also much interested in watching the fishermen at work not far from the shore. The bar at Mukah is shallow and at times very dangerous. In the season of the north-east monsoon—from November until well into March—it is impossible to reach Mukah from the sea; and although our visit took place in April, during the south-west monsoon, the water was hardly ever free from the proverbial white horses, which, however, did not deter the skilful Mukah fishermen from following their trade; for fish and sago are the staple foods of the place. Legend relates that the "fishing smacks" in which they venture themselves are their own invention from olden times, and they certainly looked funny to me. Bobbing up and down between the waves, they appeared like oval washing-tubs and I was told by the Milanoes that they are able to stand up to the heaviest sea. The boatmen dig their oars into the water and pull like mad through the trough of the surf, slew their crafts bow on and ride over the breaker. One wave gone by, they hurry on, meeting the next in the same manner, thus managing to escape catastrophe and gradually bringing their catch of fish to land. It was a great amusement to me to watch the bobbing tubs. I thought, however, that the Milanoe fishermen must be a tiny bit hen-pecked. The wives told me that the husbands had to behave themselves. If they failed to bring home a goodly provision of fish they were ruthlessly locked out until such time as they succeeded in replenishing the larders. They said they were perfectly right in behaving in this way to their husbands, as they, themselves, prepared the sago and the men must do their part about the fish.

I enjoyed our visit to Mukah in spite of the smell. Mr. de Crespigny was a most delightful man who had attained the rank of Commander in the Royal Navy, after which he had left the service. He held an appointment under the Colonial Office at Labuan, where he met my husband and decided to join his service. Our acquaintance at Mukah was the beginning of a friendship which only came to an end at his death twenty years later. He loved Sarawak and all her people, was devoted to my husband and proved one of his most valued and trusted officers.

Like all the Residents in the country, he was most hospitable and gave up the only bedrooms in the Fort to our use. On the first evening of our stay my husband and Mr. de Crespigny talked far into the night, whilst I retired early and prepared myself for bed. Although devoid of many of the most ordinary comforts of a European bedroom, my room contained a very original piece of furniture—a small cannon with its muzzle thrust through the port-hole just by my bed. As I brushed my hair, my eyes resting on the gun, I saw a large rat creeping up its rounded base. When it gained the top it sat down on its hind legs, facing me, and began to wash its face. I thought it looked quite friendly and made encouraging noises at it while I went on brushing my hair. It sat there, quite unperturbed, until I moved to get into bed, when it slowly climbed down from the gun and disappeared. I then got into bed, placing my lighted candle on a chair beside me, and, after tucking in my mosquito curtain, I settled myself to read. Presently I heard a scratching noise on the chair. No mistake! My friend the rat had come back again; and although I clapped my hands and made noises at him he would not be frightened away. In safety behind the mosquito curtain, I did not much mind, but went on reading until I heard sounds of wrestling on the chair. I looked and saw the rat attacking the lighted candle. It managed to pull it out of the socket, when it went out, there was a flop on the floor, and the rat had made off with it, a fact which I realized when I lighted a match. I stayed three nights at Mukah Fort, and each night the rat appeared on the scene and behaved in the same way.

As I did not wish to annoy anyone by complaining, I said nothing until our last morning there, when I airily mentioned to Mr. de Crespigny that the rat had found its way into the bedroom once or twice. "Oh yes," he said. " I often see him. He is quite at home there." I said no more, and remembered Robert Bruce's extreme affection for a spider !

CHAPTER XII

AFTER leaving Mukah we proceeded to Bintulu, at that time our most northern possession on the coast of Sarawak. We stayed one night at the Fort overlooking the sea. The Bintulu people all came to pay their respects, and on the occasion of the women's visit an unusual sight greeted me as I looked out through the lattice-work of the Fort, which stood on a low hill. I saw a procession of moving objects which exactly resembled conically shaped tea-trays made of red, yellow and black matting. Hundreds of them moved up the path towards the Fort, but *how* they moved I could not make out. Presently a great crowd of women arrived at the Court House, and, as usual, friendship was soon established between us. I asked them about the tea-trays whose approach had so interested me. "These are our hats, Rajah Ranee," they said. "We always wear hats like that. Would you like to have one?" I thanked them and accepted the original headgear, which I still possess. It hangs on a wall in my Cornish home. Certainly, odd as such hats look, they are a great protection against sunstroke.

Our journey back to Kuching was comfortable

enough. The sea was smooth and all went well.
I found that the children had been well cared
for during our absence, and I resumed my life
at the Astana, happy and contented. *Then,*
oh dear, oh dear!—what a bore it all was!
Another infant on its way! My husband
thought that a trip to Singapore might do me
good; so off we went; my brother, my three
babies, their English nurse, Ima and all. We
stayed for three weeks at the principal hotel in
Singapore. My husband and my brother Harry
paid a visit to the Governor-General at Buiten-
zorg, in Java, which they enjoyed immensely.
His Excellency, his staff and the Dutch they met
with proved most courteous and hospitable. I
was sorry that owing to my state of health it was
impossible for me to accompany them. Meanwhile, the Governor of Singapore, Sir Harry
Orde, and his wife and Sir Benson and Lady
Maxwell were most kind to me, as were all our
acquaintances living there. I always loved Singapore and thought it a very privileged place by
reason of its charming residents. I then first
met Frank Swettenham, who became a close
friend, and whom I regard (as everyone must who
knows of his splendid work in the Straits) as one
of the really great men of the British Empire.

On the return journey to Kuching, as I was
crossing my cabin in the dark, I fell down a
hatchway, which had been left open through the
carelessness of the steward. I hurt myself some-

what and had to be pulled up almost by the hair
of my head. When, on our arrival, Mrs. Helms
heard of the accident, she became most pessimistic,
and Datu Isa was also much perturbed. However, I felt no ill effects at the time; but two
months later, during one of the Rajah's absences
on the coast, my baby arrived prematurely—
still-born. I was really very ill, I believe at the
point of death. The doctor ran about the garden
between treatment and paroxysms. The English
nurse, being a spinster inexperienced in maternity
cases, was of no use, while the Malay midwife
sat by my bed, thumping her head on the floor
and screaming out " Mati, mati! " (dead, dead)
at the top of her voice. A despatch boat was
sent to warn the Rajah and hasten his home-
coming. Such a fuss there was, and how pleased
I should have been could I have realized it at
the time; for at last I had become an important
personage in the world of Sarawak. I imagine
that, in their heart of hearts, the English residents
in Kuching must have rather enjoyed the excitement caused by my illness—all except my brother,
for we were devoted to one another.

Then a very touching incident occurred. A
portion of the Astana grounds had been set aside
and consecrated, some years previously, as a
cemetery for one or two of the Brooke family
who were buried there. My poor baby not
having been christened, the Bishop vetoed the
idea of his finding his tiny grave in so holy a spot.

The Datus, on hearing this, were so indignant at such a state of things that, although good Mohammedans, they came to the Astana, laid the poor mite in a coffin and carried it themselves to the cemetery, where it was buried with affection and dignity. How I loved and honoured them for their kind and broad-minded action !

When the Rajah returned I was very ill, the doctor being still under grave apprehensions. Men and women who are known to be of a silent and undemonstrative nature are often wrongly accused of heartlessness. My husband felt my alarming illness most keenly. He would sit alone on the verandah for hours, awaiting developments, and those who knew him well noticed that during the few anxious days when I was at my worst his hair became much greyer than before. After all, it was the Rajah himself who turned the scales in my favour. He bethought himself of beef-tea reinforced with a good dose of brandy. He came to my room, raised my head and gently poured a small quantity, drop by drop, down my throat. The effect was wonderful. After days of utter prostration, I began to revive and waggle about. " Oh, Charlie," I whispered, " what a good chap you are ! " " Charlie," delighted, fed me with a few more drops of the stuff every hour or so ; and the doctor, appearing from some room below in the Astana and seeing my improvement, said, " So glad, Rajah, that you have

followed my prescription." Lucky he was that
his untruthful boast did not strike him dead,
for he had never even *thought* of such a remedy.
Anyhow, from that time I continued to progress
and made quite a good recovery.

I had spent nearly four years in Sarawak,
during which time I had ushered four infants
into the world. Knowing that such rapid increase
to the population in an enervating climate was
trying to the health of any woman, my husband
decided that I ought to have a complete change
for a year or so, and arranged for our return to
England. So, that autumn, we embarked on
the P. and O. liner " Hydaspes " from Singapore,
in which city we had to stay for two nights at the
house of a friend. Cholera was raging there at the
time, but we were all (my husband, my brother,
the three babies, their English nurse, my maid
and myself) in good health until we reached
Aden. From that day on the most frightful
tragedies occurred. During the short period
of three days our children were all attacked by
cholera ; they died within a few hours and were
buried in the Red Sea. . . . Of what use would
it be for me to attempt to describe our feelings
at such a time ? All who have lost their children
can realize the hopelessness and misery of it all.
Poor wee mites who had done nothing but fill
a mother's heart with devotion, love and dreams
for their fair future ! There it all was. Those
flowers of beauty and loveliness mown down in a

few hours, torn from us and cast into the sea. . . .
I can say no more. But I recall, after these
many years, the kindness and sympathy we
met with from every man, woman and child on
board. I can never forget it. From the captain
down to his crew. In my experience the world
is full of kindliness and humanity. All through
that terrible time, notwithstanding his own grief
and sorrow, my husband's thoughts were centred
on me. Feeling that a prolonged stay on the
vessel would be painful for me, he sent the servants
on to England by sea, while he, my brother and
myself landed at Alexandria and made our way
to Cairo. There we sternly went about sight-see-
ing—after all the best thing we could do—with
sorrow gnawing at our hearts. My husband
and my brother Harry helped me to pull myself
together. As we go through life we realize
that sorrow and grief can be made to teach us
that our greatest duty is that of consoling those
around us. I did my best to be interested in
the Pyramids; while the Sphinx (then buried
up to its neck in sand) was strangely appealing
to me. I spent many hours gazing at the mystery.
What did it mean? Why was it put there so
many thousand years ago? A sort of terror and
ghastly hilarity seems to ooze from its face—and
yet, behind it all, cannot one trace kindness?
Kindness that unlocks the doors of discontent;
of muddlings in religions; of everything! But
there—I am stupid! Let it go at that.

Leaving the Sphinx and the Pyramids, that in a certain way had power to help in keeping me in a sane frame of mind, and forcing myself to try to face things as they were, we continued our journey to England, where my husband, my brother and myself stayed for some days at an hotel in London.

CHAPTER XIII

THE Rajah, alas! felt very bored. He knew no one, and had never felt inclined to belong to any club. Sir Harry Keppel, whom he had known intimately during piratical expeditions in Borneo, was absent from England; and, with the exception of a visit or two to the Foreign Office to consult with the Big Wigs, he had nothing to help him while away the days. Reserved and rather shy, he kept himself to himself and time hung heavy on his hands. It is not to be wondered at, therefore, that the poor dear hated London.

I was much in want of winter clothes. Never having a penny to spend on myself, and my husband being imbued with the Eastern idea that women should never go out alone, he insisted on accompanying me on my shopping excursions, paying on the nail for all my purchases and grumbling all the while at the expense. As he would not countenance the running up of bills, and private dressmakers could not be induced to receive money on the spot, I had to buy my clothes ready-made. I managed to wheedle out of him two day dresses, a best dress—for visits and Sundays—and one evening gown, not low, but with a modest V neck! All off the peg, and very horrible indeed they were. When it came to the question of a necessary fur coat I felt that my Waterloo had been reached. Oh! that fur coat I had set my heart on. What manœuvrings did I not go through till it became mine! One day a heavenly inspiration visited me. " Oh, Charlie," I said. " You know you mean to hunt this winter, and driving with you to the meets I should be so chilly without a fur coat." " Why not a good stout tweed?" said he. "Much cheaper and it would do just as well." Then evidently the idea occurred to him that as he was spending a good deal of money on himself in buying hunters, it might not be so unreasonable after all to spend a little on me. So the fur coat was bought and all was well. Extraordinary as his attitude towards his wife will appear, it must be remembered that my husband had lived abroad from the time he was thirteen, when he joined the Navy, and after his twenty-second year, when he left the Service, his life had been passed almost entirely in Sarawak. Also, in those days married women had no rights whatever in the disposal of their fortune. Luckily, I fully realized all this at the time and was greatly amused by his parsimonious views on the subject of his wife's wardrobe. I used to laugh at him sometimes until I cried. " Oh dear, Charlie," I would say. " I can't go out in my chemise!" He did not like it, but I said it all the same. So good for him, I thought. Difficulties poured in over every article of my toilet. He thought the purchase of more than one hat a reckless extravagance; while boots, shoes, stockings, gloves and linen were the subjects of more hagglings. I did have a time! When I now look back on it all I remember with satisfaction that I never confided my monetary troubles to any of my friends. They simply would not have understood such a state of things. I knew my husband's nature and could make proper allowance for him, and I should have felt it disloyal to discuss his queer ideas with anyone, however closely related. He was fond of me and always spoke kindly— sometimes even admiringly—about me to his entourage. And, when all was said and done, it was really very comic!

The great question at that time in my husband's mind was the finding of a suitable house in a good hunting county for the winter, and, as I had many friends in Wiltshire, he eventually decided to rent Sir Hungerford Pollen's place at Rodbourne, about three miles distant from Malmesbury and within easy reach of the Duke of Beaufort's and the V. W. H. hounds.

Sir Hungerford was kindness itself to us when we visited him at his invitation so as to decide whether his house would suit us. Since the death of his wife he had made his home with his two sisters, Miss Louisa and Miss Jessie Pollen, who had brought up his young family of two sons and five daughters as only their own mother could have done. At the period of which I write he was about to marry again, and his family, devoted as they were to their two aunts, refused to leave them, and moved with them to a farm-house close to Rodbourne.

This was the beginning of a most delightful friendship. Sir Hungerford's eldest daughter was about my own age and we young people were always together, Aunt Louie and Aunt Jessie also taking me under their wing. The Rajah was in his element, having bought four hunters, a pair of ponies and a pony carriage for me, also four quite untamed horses which he used to drive on non-hunting days. He was generally alone on his drives, as none of us could be induced to venture ourselves behind his unbroken team, the leaders having a playful way of turning round and looking at him at odd moments, or upsetting the coach in ditches, my husband miraculously escaping destruction at each mishap. Through the dear Pollens we made some of the most delightful friends, and I also saw quite a lot of my grandfather's widow, Mrs. Willes Johnson, and all her young unmarried daughters. I was very happy to be among people of my own age and I always recall those days with the greatest pleasure. We sewed, embroidered, sketched, painted and played the piano. What fun it all was! I was sad when the winter came to an end. By that time another infant was on its way. I went and told Aunt Louie and cried on her shoulder. She was tender and discreet. " Think of your country, my child," she said. " How hopeless it would be if your husband had no heir." And she gently went on talking me into resignation. She was a darling and I loved her.

When my husband heard the news he thought the best plan would be to take a house in London so that I could be within reach of a good doctor. So, having arranged with Sir Hungerford to re-rent Rodbourne for the following winter, he set out to hunt for a London abode and settled on a roomy, comfortably furnished house in Queen Street, Mayfair, where we established ourselves with our servants. Alas! the question of drains had never entered the poor man's head. Dreadful things were discovered in that most important of all quarters; doctors and sanitary men were called in, with the result that we were ordered to leave at once, which we did without delay. We found rooms at 31, Albemarle Street, where —to proceed quickly with my narrative—my son Vyner, now Rajah of Sarawak, was born on the 21st of September, 1874. His arrival was a great source of joy and consolation to us both. He was a healthy, beautiful baby ; and congratulations poured in from all our friends in Wiltshire and, later on, from Sarawak.

In those days doctors and midwives were not so punctilious as they are now in guarding against contingencies, and although both the doctor and my elderly nurse had been told of my inability to produce proper food, the child was born without their having made any provision for its sustenance. The doctor advised artificial feeding, when, to the astonishment of all concerned, my husband emphatically declared that no child of his should be subjected to such treatment, and insisted that a wet nurse should be found forthwith. The doctor, after a few hours' search, succeeded in obtaining the wished-for female, a poor young thing who had given birth to an illegitimate baby, which baby, the doctor assured us, was being cared for by competent persons. All went well for the moment, the doctor having satisfied himself on all counts, and my infant passed a happy peaceful night in the arms of his nourishment giver.

Next morning, however, a bolt from the blue descended on us in the shape of a legal summons for the newly-established nurse to appear before the coroner concerning the death of her own baby, which had occurred the previous night. My husband was naturally somewhat upset, but he determined to see the poor woman through her trouble, and took her in a cab to the Court. After considerable delay the case was heard and the protectors of the baby exonerated, as it was proved that the child had accidentally been overlain. When the matter was at last all cleared up, my husband, who had been chafing at the slowness of the proceedings, stood up in Court and declared that it was scandalous that his child should be kept all this time without food owing to its nurse's time being wasted on so obviously absurd a charge as being concerned in any way with the death of her own infant! When he had finished, a woman in the body of the Court was heard to say, " 'Ark at 'im carrying on. Shouldn't wonder but 'e was the father of the pore girl's biby an' 'ad 'im put aht o' the wiy. Shime!" Needless to say, my husband paid no attention but hurried the girl out of Court, into a cab and home to his hungry little son.

After this excitement everything went smoothly. The young woman did her duty nobly, was well looked after and kindly cared for by us all and got over her sorrows in happier surroundings when she returned with us to Rodbourne in the autumn.

My second winter there was as delightful as the first. The Rajah hunted three or four days a week and was perfectly happy driving his coach and breaking-in his horses. The Pollens and I continued to enjoy our rather mid-Victorian pursuits and the society of many charming friends. Certainly our trip to England had done us both good.

When the time came for us to leave Rodbourne I cried a lot. Females of that era were all that way inclined. Indeed I notice in a tome recently published, *The Prince Consort and his Brother*, that the Good are frequently given to tears!

And I have come to the conclusion that the health of the present-day woman must suffer quite considerably by the elimination of so potent a method of consolation as " a good cry."

At the time of our return to Sarawak, as my son was then only six months old and not yet weaned, we left him with his nurse, in the care of Bishop MacDougall and his wife, very dear friends of the first Rajah Brooke, and consoled ourselves as best we could for not being able to have him with us by the knowledge that he could not have been in better hands. We sailed from Marseilles in April and had a comfortable and uneventful passage. On arriving at Singapore we spent a couple of days with the newly-appointed Governor, his wife and charming daughters, after which we embarked in the " Heartsease " for Sarawak. Arrived at Kuching we were welcomed with the greatest affection by everyone, and when all the greetings of the Europeans and officials were over and my dear Malay friends appeared in shoals at tea-time, I felt that the happiest moment of our return had arrived. Dear Datu Isa and I seated once more under the trees in the Astana garden, while on the grass at our feet sat the younger married women and the virgins. All as it used to be ! " And how was Mem Queen ? " inquired Datu Isa with intense interest. (She meant Queen Victoria.) " And what did Mem Queen say to you ? " For reasons best known to myself I fenced beauti-

fully with these questions. I replied with truth
(for I had been to Court) that I had seen " Mem
Queen " and that she had smiled graciously
upon me, as that Greatest of all Ladies was wont
to do to all those who paid her homage. Datu
Isa then took hold of my hand, held it between
her own, sighed and looked down. She had
evidently been trying, by her questions about
" Mem Queen," to mitigate the pain of our first
meeting and my home-coming to the empty
nurseries of the Astana. Then she looked up
and smiled. " And our Rajah Muda," she said.
" When does he come to Sarawak ? " When she
heard that he was in the care of Bishop and Mrs.
MacDougall, whom she had known well in
bygone years, she brightened up considerably,
and beamed with joy when she heard that in a
very few months the child would be brought
out under careful supervision to Sarawak and his
own people.

CHAPTER XIV

SHORTLY after our return the Rajah decided to visit the Barram River, taking with him Mr. de Crespigny, the Borneo Company's Agent, my brother and myself. The territory which he intended to explore was situated further north than Sarawak's most northerly possession, Bintulu, in Borneo, and was still at that time ruled over by the Sultan of Brunei.

Now the tribe inhabiting the regions at the head of the Barram River were called Kayans, and were much given to foraging about and falling foul of Dyaks and other tribes who were subjects of the Rajah. As the Sultan of Brunei appeared to be powerless to control these Kayans and the outbreaks of hostilities were becoming all too frequent, the Rajah decided to go there, get in touch with the offending tribe and try to bring about a better state of things for everybody concerned, but especially for his own people who were being so constantly harassed. I don't believe he quite knew what he would find there or what he was going to do, but he realized that the Kayans were badly governed and out of control, and would probably be glad to do as so many other tribes had done and become his subjects.

Whatever was in the Rajah's mind, we all knew better than to ask him any questions. Had one of us attempted to do so the offender would no doubt have speedily found himself (or herself!) seated in one of the dinghies of the " Heartsease " being borne rapidly back to Kuching. Therefore as we sped on our journey, the sea being calm, we talked of shoes and ships and sealing-wax, of cabbages and kings, but *never* of the object of our quest. All that the Rajah vouchsafed to Mr. de Crespigny, when we were at breakfast that first day, was that he was taking me with him in order to impress upon the inhabitants of the Barram River district that his mission was a peaceful one, to which information we answered " Oh ! " and went on eating. Funnily enough, the prospect of a journey into unknown and savage country, peopled by totally ungovernable tribes, had no terror for me, so absolutely confident was I in my husband's ability to deal with blood-thirsty and uncivilized offenders. Sometimes I almost longed for a slight spice of danger in such, to me, novel undertakings. But no! I always felt perfectly safe !

When we arrived at the mouth of the hitherto unexplored Barram, members of the crew were sent off in ship's boats to take soundings, to enable us to enter its uncharted waters. After hours of testing, when I saw at each dip the sounding poles standing high above the water-mark with only a depth of two or three feet even at high tide, I began to despair, and think that we might be kept examining the shallow entrance for days or even weeks, for I knew that the Rajah's patience was infinite and that he would not be turned back from accomplishing the purpose he had in view. There he sat with his three men companions, all smoking their horrible Manila cigars and staring at the unknown coast, debating about the possibilities of future trade in the fertile country inland. How little then did my husband foresee the benefits which would be conferred on Sarawak's revenues in years to come by the discovery of the vast oil-fields on the sandy shores they gazed at from the deck of the " Heartsease."

At last, after many hours, shouts of triumph were heard from the exploring boats. The men waved their oars in the air; a channel had been found. But, alas, the yacht could not make her way in owing to her overdraught of water. However, the Borneo Company's steamer, " Sri Sarawak," which had accompanied the " Heartsease " in view of such a contingency, being able to negotiate the shallows, we all transferred into it, and slowly, very slowly, and with the greatest care at the steering wheel, found ourselves over the bar and at last inside the river. The " Heartsease " was left outside at anchor, and we crawled along with infinite caution on our way up-

stream. Mr. de Crespigny, pencil and paper
in hand, seated himself on the bridge in order
to make a chart as the quartermaster called out
his soundings. Up and up we went. Now and
then, beyond the vast forest lands, we would
get glimpses of mountains blue in the distance.
At first the course of the river was pretty straight.
Then it began to wiggle and waggle in and out
of its many bends, giving Mr. de Crespigny and
his pencil a good deal of work. We were making
for a somewhat important village called Batu
Gading (Ivory Rock), which, the Rajah had
been told by some of his Kayan subjects near
Kuching, stood a good way up. We passed
several villages, whose long houses made of palm
leaves with wooden walls were propped up by
posts which at high tide stood in the water.
Men, women and children were moving about,
some of them pounding rice on the broad
verandahs, while others paddled themselves about
in canoes. They betrayed no surprise at the
appearance of what, to them, was a hitherto
unknown object—a ship with a smoking funnel
steaming up their river. The Rajah pulled out
his handkerchief and waved it repeatedly as we
passed each village, bidding us all do the same.
The natives waved to us in return. We were
getting along nicely and my husband was enjoying himself. That evening we anchored off
one of these villages, but no sign of life appeared
outside. As night came on and the sky was

filled with stars, the most awful wails and shrieks
began to issue from the wooden walls of the one
long house which constituted the village. A
corpse was lying inside and they were wailing
for their dead. We had to stay where we had
anchored as it was too dark for us to proceed,
but what a gruesome night we spent! Even
when we hauled up anchor at daybreak the wailing
was still going on. " Ah, yes," said Mr. de
Crespigny cheerily, as we steamed away, " in
the midst of life we are in death ! " The Rajah,
who knew most of the customs of the different
peoples of those parts, thought it likely that they
belonged to a tribe called Muruts, whose custom
it is on death occasions for the females to sit on
the verandah opposite the room of the departed,
cover their heads with cloths, and wail and moan,
while the men visit each other and drink. The
heads of the near female relations of the corpse
are then shaved, after which the deceased is
pushed into a large jar, the top is closed down and
the jar is then covered with red cloth edged with
tinsel. In the case of a chief ten years may
elapse before the jar is buried in their graveyard,
the ceremony being accompanied by much firing
of guns and many rejoicings. In the interval
between the death and the burial, the jar is
placed on a wooden platform, erected a few yards
from the house. My brother wished that he
could have had a peep at the ceremony, unknown
to the people, but I thought it all very grue-

some and was thankful to get away from the scene.

We continued our slow progress for three whole days, after which we began to wonder whether we should ever reach our goal. Even the Rajah showed slight signs of impatience. At last, at sunset on the fourth day, on turning a sharp bend we saw a great steep rock sticking out of the bed of the river near the shore. Along the bank by the water stood a very long house on poles, covering the bank for about a quarter of a mile. Evidently the village of a very large tribe. It was to us a welcome sight. We had evidently arrived. Many canoes, large and small, were tied up to posts, but there was a deserted look along the banks and on the terrace of the house (or village). After some time we made out through our field-glasses a group of some fifty or sixty men emerging from the forest near by and making their way to the house. Splendid fellows they were, with spears and shields and warlike accoutrements. Their caps bristled with hornbill plumes, their hair looked as though glued down their backs, their ears, weighted down by leaden earrings, hung down to their shoulders, while the upper part was studded with tiger-cats' teeth which looked like reversed horns. Some of their armlets were of ivory, and dozens of bangles covered their arms and legs. Their jackets were made of hide; their chawats twisted round their waists, taking the place of drawers, ended in a drapery front and back. Their sword sheaths were decorated with feathers and brass; they held spears in their hands. The whole effect was warlike, formidable and very picturesque. Both my husband and Mr. de Crespigny were of the opinion that they had just returned from some head-hunting expedition in the neighbourhood. They paid no attention whatever to the steamer, but quietly passed it by and made their way up the forty-foot bamboo giving entrance to the house and disappeared inside. Silence followed. The river ran past us to the sea. Night was coming on, and there we were in a wilderness of wood and water—not a sound to be heard. "What do you think of it, de Crespigny?" said my husband at dinner. "I think, Rajah, there must be Brunei influence at work, and, with your permission, I will call on the Chief at the house to-morrow and inform him that you wish to see him on board." The Rajah approved of this suggestion and Mr. de Crespigny was accordingly rowed ashore next morning. He was about to climb the pole to the house when three Kayans appeared at the top of it and waved to him to proceed no further. The three Kayans then came down the ladder, fully armed with spears and swords, and as they reached the ground Mr. de Crespigny took hold of each in turn and pushed him into the boat. They made no resistance and soon found themselves in the presence of the Rajah on the deck

of the " Sri Sarawak." They were fine-looking
men, fairer and stouter than the Dyaks, all in
full war-paint, and quiet and dignified in their
greetings to the Rajah and myself when we
touched the tips of each other's fingers. The
conversation, interpreted by Mr. de Crespigny,
was something like this, the Chief of the
village being the spokesman. " Rajah Sarawak
he very big man. Why he come here ? " " I
have come to pay you a visit," said the Rajah.
" When can I go to your house ? " " Oh,
Rajah—very sad," was the reply. " Rajah cannot
come in just now. House is ' permali ' " (under
a curse). " No one from outside can come in for
days." " Then I will wait until days pass,"
said the Rajah in a quiet and determined way.
The Chief said nothing, but looked down and
scratched himself. The Rajah then said, " Have
you any strangers staying with you now ? "
The Chief looked uncomfortable and then replied,
" Yes, there are two Malays, sent from the Sultan,
but they are ' permali ' too. They are shut up—
they must not leave the house." " Very well,"
said my husband. " Now you may go." The
trio then took their departure after once more
touching the tips of our fingers. They went down
the companion, were rowed ashore in the boat,
went up the bamboo ladder into the house and
disappeared. " The Sultan of Brunei must have
been told of my intended visit here," said the
Rajah. " But here I remain until I get into the

village and have a talk with the people." What rather puzzled my husband and Mr. de Crespigny, however, was the fact of the inhabitants having resorted to the " permali," so that no strangers should be allowed to enter the walls of the house.

I rather forget how many days we remained at anchor in the river below the long house at Batu Gading. It may have been three, or possibly four. Even the Kayans themselves, I imagine, were aware that despite the two Brunei emissaries and their ruse of prolonging the " permali," nothing they could say or do would induce the Rajah to leave the district until his purpose— that of visiting the village—had been accomplished. Thus it happened that one morning the Rajah, tired of waiting, determined to send the " permali " and all its measures to the devil. He ordered Mr. de Crespigny and my brother to land forthwith, make their way up the pole to the house, and enter it with or without permission. Now it must be remembered that, in their heart of hearts, the Kayans knew the Rajah to be friendly to their tribe, and were only held back from welcoming him by the presence of the envoys from the Sultan of Brunei. I wish I could have seen the famous meeting ! Mr. de Crespigny, urbane, dignified, very quiet in gesture and able to speak the Kayan language. My brother, young, lively, full of mischief and fun as he smiled and winked and showed signs of

friendliness to the young Kayan warriors. My
brother had a *way* with him which in all his
journeys among the natives of Sarawak awakened
friendly response in their hearts. It must have
been apparent to the Kayans (themselves fully
armed with spears and parangs) that they were
in the presence of two brave men, for neither Mr.
de Crespigny nor my brother had thought it
necessary to protect themselves even with walking-
sticks. " Now, you men of Batu Gading," said
Mr. de Crespigny, addressing the Chief, his
followers and the two Pangerans, who hovered
in the background. " The Rajah of Sarawak
has come to pay you a friendly visit and, as you
are aware, he is not accustomed to be kept waiting.
Therefore, to-day, at the hour before the sun
begins to set, his Ranee and himself intend to
pay you a visit. He expects you—' permali ' or
no—to be in readiness to receive him at that
time." At the conclusion of this speech Mr. de
Crespigny and my brother took their departure,
escorted to the entrance of the house by the
Chief and some of his men, descended the notched
bamboo, and returned to the ship. They had not
failed to note that their announcement of the
Rajah's visit was received by the Sultan's Pangerans with evidences of the utmost discontent.

As eight bells sounded from the deck of the
" Sri Sarawak " that afternoon, the ship's boat,
with crew reinforced by four of the Rajah's
guard with loaded muskets, was awaiting us at

the companion ; my husband and I, accompanied by Mr. de Crespigny and my brother, got in and were rowed ashore. Lo and behold ! the landing-stage was filled with Kayan warriors, the Chief and his men ranged along the bank on either side of the climbing-pole. And how picturesque they did look, bristling with swords, spears, feathered caps, tigers' teeth ; tattooed on legs and arms, be-bangled and hung with beads. I thought them beautiful and loved them all. As we stepped on shore the Rajah, with an impressive wave of the arm, ordered the boat, its entire crew, also the armed guard, back to the " Sri Sarawak." " No guard whatever, Rajah ? " inquired Mr. de Crespigny, as the boat receded from the shore. " A sign that we trust them absolutely," said my husband, as the rifles were borne off on the stream. After they had saluted each other, the Chief led the way up the bamboo, followed by the Rajah. Then my turn came. Oh dear, another such a getting upstairs ! Seeing my rueful expression, two beautiful young Kayan warriors came forward and offered me a hand. They were so graceful and charming I did my very best. They smiled sweetly at each effort I made to turn out my toes to the required position. They reminded me of Pan and other sylvan gods I had read about in fairy tales. When we reached the top each one deposited my hand back by my side with a courtly gesture. So many years gone by since then, and I can see them now! How I enjoyed it all, so strange, novel and fascinating was the scene I had been pushed into!

The Rajah, still escorted by the Chief and the most important members of the tribe, was the first to enter the long house (capable, said Mr. de Crespigny, of holding some five hundred people). There was a platform in front, open to the air, and the verandah along which we were escorted was roofed-in the whole length of the house. As I followed my husband, Mr. de Crespigny and my brother on either side of me, I saw, all ranged against the wooden wall dividing the verandah from the dwelling-rooms beyond, Kayan warriors, spears in hand, standing straight and immovable. No one spoke. There was no sound but our footsteps as we were being led . . . where? At last we found ourselves in a large room the floor of which was covered with beautiful mats but having no furniture of any kind except two large blocks of wood about three feet high, covered with some yellow cotton material. These were placed in readiness for the Rajah and myself to sit on, with our backs to the light. I was afterwards told by Mr. de Crespigny that the seat occupied by the Rajah was a huge slab cut out of the Tapang tree, those seats being heir-looms in Kayan families and descending, black with age, from fathers to sons for many genera-tions. Mine was no doubt an afterthought of no great consequence. Mr. de Crespigny and my

brother seated themselves on the floor. For a
long time we all sat on in silence, the only sounds
to be heard being a cough or two now and then—
the sort of coughs to be heard frequently at
gatherings where constraint is felt and people are
ill at ease. The behaviour of the two Pangerans
from Brunei was somewhat disconcerting. They
kept prowling about among the Kayans, making
signs to them and looking askance at us, until
they finally wormed their way over to where we
were and seated themselves on the floor behind
us. Most uncomfortable! I remember wonder-
ing if they intended jabbing us unprotected ones
in the back with a kris! Admirable as usual on
such occasions, my husband sat on, apparently
as unconcerned as though he were seated on a
chair in his study at home. He pulled his
moustache, looked around at the assembly and
then said, " I have come to see you all as a friend.
I want to open up trade on this river between
my people and yours." The Malay envoys
hated it all, became restive and kept on chewing
sirih, but the Chief and his followers were
evidently pleased. The shy coughings ceased
and gave place to contented wriggles of their
bodies as they sat on the floor. After a little,
the Chief rose to his feet and gave tongue. Being
ignorant of the Kayan language, the sounds he
produced seemed to me like the croakings of a
demented frog, but I was told that what he said
was: " Rajah Sarawak, big man, friend of

Kayans all over the country. Rajah wish make friends. We wish too!" "Baik!" (Good) replied my husband, and everyone, except the two emissaries of the Sultan, seemed to feel they were getting along very well. Smiles and greetings were exchanged, and a comfortable feeling came over us all. Then even poor me had a brain-wave! I turned to Mr. de Crespigny. "Ask the Chief where all the women are. I have come here with the Rajah, and as yet not one woman have I seen." "Not a bad idea," said the Rajah. "Tell the Chief to send for the women." A young Kayan went off hurriedly, opened a door leading from the hall where we were sitting, went within and closed the door. Presently it was flung open, and a charming procession of females made their way into the hall, headed by the Chief's wife, one of the most picturesque figures I have ever beheld. Small of stature, exquisitely formed, with a pale yellow complexion and large dark eyes of a somewhat Mongolian shape, the wonderful creature made her way slowly and with dignity to where we were sitting. Her black hair hung down over her shoulders and was bound round with a gleaming fillet of straw, her petticoat of white cotton was draped round her waist and reached her ankles, being slit up on one side to allow freedom of movement. At first I thought that her leg, which was revealed as she walked, was encased in dark blue velvet, but when she came nearer me I saw that what I had taken to be velvet was a tattoo pattern covering her feet and legs. Behind her walked with equal dignity about thirty women, old and young. They appeared to me like Greek goddesses about to perform some sacred rite. The Chief's wife came up to me, took possession of my hand which I placed in both of hers; we smiled at each other and it seemed as though mutual liking and trust were at once established between us. I was wearing a thin gold chain on which hung a coral charm someone had once brought me from Naples. I pulled it off and slipped it over her head. More smiles, more messages of good-will flashed from each other's eyes—those true indexes to innermost feelings. She sat on the floor at my feet, affectionately patting my knee with one hand while with the other she lovingly fondled the little charm I had hung round her neck. "A good idea of yours, Ranee," said Mr. de Crespigny. The Rajah, too, seemed pleased, but of course he said nothing. I loved approbation, for I got so very little, and I felt important with a modest place in the picture. My brother was too much occupied on his own account to pay any attention to me. He was always at home in any company—civilized or no—and was then busily engaged with a young Kayan, a son of the Chief, inserting stilettos into each other's arms and mixing their blood, thus proclaiming to all and sundry that they had become

brothers and were cementing their new relation-
ship in this manner. " Quite the right thing to
do," said Mr. de Crespigny, who, however, did
not show the slightest eagerness to join in the
scratchings by stilettos.

When the Rajah gave the signal for us to depart, the women all escorted me to the entrance
pole. The problem of descending was even
worse than that of ascending, but helped by my
graceful Kayan cavaliers I accomplished it safely.
The people all took leave of us with great affection, imploring us to come again, and we were
rowed out to the " Sri Sarawak," followed by the
most vociferous farewells from the entire village
gathered at the landing-stage. By that time the
Brunei agents were no more to be seen !

" We must weigh anchor and move off at
daybreak," said the Rajah, " or else the people
will imagine that they must keep on sending us
tokens of their goodwill and affection." So, at
the first streak of dawn, we steamed our way
back down the Barram, all in the best of tempers.
Thanks to Mr. de Crespigny's valuable chart
taken on the way up, our trip back to the mouth
of the river was accomplished in a much shorter
time. In the evenings after dinner, Mr. de
Crespigny told me a great deal about the Kayans
and their rites and beliefs, all of which interested
me intensely. " They have their god of life,
their god of storm—of fire—of harvest, lakes and
rivers. Also a god who conducts the souls of the

dead to Hades. Did you not see," said he,
" that tree in front of the house, with its branches
buried in the ground and its roots upturned ? "
I had indeed remarked it but had not said anything for fear of asking too many questions.
" Well," he continued, " it is supposed to form a
ladder of communication between the earth and
any friendly god. Fire is also a means of spiritual
communication, prayers being offered when anything—even a cigarette—is set alight. The gods
of war, of life, of harvest, of fire are all the friends
of man." " But don't they sometimes send their
prayers to their gods through certain birds ? "
I asked. " Certainly," was the reply. " They
look upon the carrion hawk, for instance, as a
specially important messenger, while other birds,
by their hooting or cries, are supposed to direct
the people on their way to war and give them
guidance and warning in their farming and their
home-life." " What a pity it is," said I, " that
they take such delight in that disgusting custom
of theirs, head-taking ! Chopping off their
enemies' heads, taking them home and dangling
them from their ceilings and bed-posts ! " " Well,
after all," said Mr. de Crespigny, with a gentle—
I might almost say an indulgent—smile, " there
is a good deal of chivalrous courtesy manifested
in even those apparently bloodthirsty transactions.
Doesn't history tell us that in Britain itself, before
the days of the Norman invasion, warriors were
known to quaff bumpers of wine from the skulls

of fallen foes ? The knife of a guillotine is not more swift than the parang of the Kayan or Dyak. Nor are their trophies ever treated with insults or disrespect, but are carried home to their villages by the conquerors with the greatest care, given important places in their houses and addressed each day by members of the tribe. Food is laid before them on small wooden ledges, and a fire is kept perpetually burning so that they shall not feel cold. Moreover, their captors look forward to meeting them in the next world as their servants or helpers, without sign of ill-will on either side." " Dear me ! " said I, " how friendly—and even beautiful—war seems to be out here," remembering with admiration the splendid Kayan warriors in the long house we had just left. One night the Rajah suddenly appeared on the scene. Unknown to us, he had overheard part of our conversation. " You have given the Ranee the wrong idea of the whole thing, de Crespigny," he said severely. " And why ? " " It goes in at one ear and out at the other ! " " Oh no, Charlie," I said. " Mr. de Crespigny has been lovely ! I did enjoy his talk." " Well, well," said my husband, " you had better get off to bed, and don't go dreaming of Kayans and head-takings ! "

It was morning when we found ourselves at the mouth of the Barram. A capful of wind was blowing from the south-west and Mr. de Crespigny seemed rather perturbed about our chances of getting out to the " Heartsease " in such weather, but the Rajah appeared quite calm. I sometimes think that my husband's wonderful success as ruler, law-maker, civilizer and so forth may have been partly due to his never allowing " ifs " and " might be's " to interfere with his plans. On this particular occasion he was probably perfectly well aware, as a Naval man, that the vagaries of the strong wind might delay our boarding the yacht for a day, or even two or three days, but he never allowed anyone to assume that there was any anxiety in his mind on the subject. So we fussed and packed according to his orders. On arriving at the last reach of the river and coming into full view of the sea, the gale increased in force and great walls of white surf breaking on the shallow sandy shores threatened annihilation to any ship reckless enough to attempt to cross the bar. The Rajah, field-glass in hand, examined the position and ordered the anchor to be dropped. " Well, de Crespigny, we *are* stuck here for to-night," he said, and relapsed into silence. Presently, from where I had gone to be out of the wind, I heard the captain, the steward and, I think, the cook expressing their anxiety about the depleted state of the larder. They had provisioned the " Sri Sarawak " amply for the trip but had not reckoned on the extra days of waiting up at Batu Gading (owing to the " permali " !), which had strained her resources, and we had had just enough to last us till that morning,

by which time we had expected to be aboard the
"Heartsease." From what I could make out,
there appeared to be nothing to fall back upon
but dozens of tins of biscuits and dozens of pots
of strawberry jam. On looking around us as
we stood on deck, we had seen several wild cattle
roaming about near the sandy shore of the river.
The sight of these tawny creatures filled two or
three of our party on board with the happy idea
of providing some solid meals while at the same
time satisfying their sporting instincts. Rifles
were pulled out, ammunition procured, and off
the men set in a dinghy for the shore, watched
with interest by Mr. de Crespigny and myself
through our field-glasses, he expatiating on the
satisfying meal which no doubt we should be
enjoying before long. About half an hour after
the hunters had disappeared round some green
shrubs near the shore, we suddenly saw them
emerge, running for their lives, pursued by an
infuriated animal that looked like a great bull.
The excitement was intense, and they just managed
to reach the boat and push off in time, returning
very much quicker than they had set out!
Poor dears, they looked very discomfited as they
silently came on board. "Yes," said the Rajah,
"I thought that might happen; the cattle on
these beaches are known to be savage and dangerous." So there we were! For two whole days
while we were waiting for the wind to die down,
our meals consisted of biscuits and strawberry

jam, eked out by smaller and smaller portions of white bread made from the last of the flour. The men consoled themselves with mild potations of beer and brandy-and-soda and I drank tea, of which we luckily still had plenty.

Yet, through it all, good temper reigned supreme. Such silly jokes we indulged in ! I pinned up Mr. de Crespigny's waistcoat with a safety-pin, which pin, he gallantly assured me, he would treasure for ever ! We weighed each other on the weighing machine, pretending that we became lighter and lighter on the biscuits and jam diet. All very innocent, very silly, but such good fun ! When at last the storm died down and we reached the " Heartsease " to begin our journey back to Kuching, I, for one, felt sorry to think that our happy adventures had come to an end.

CHAPTER XV

AFTER all is said and done, although I often received letters from friends in England expressing commiseration about my removal from a civilized world, my time in Sarawak was quite agreeably spent among the daily happenings going on around me. My beloved friends, the Malay women, occasional visits from so-called head-seekers from up-river districts, the strange birds—nameless in English parlance—frequenting our garden. The oddest things happened—like things in a dream—and one came to look upon them as the usual occurrences of everyday life. One evening, when walking in the garden, I saw one of our gardeners, who was deaf and dumb, lying across the path, one of his ankles swollen the size of a leg of mutton; a tiny black spot in the middle of the swelling showed me that a snake had been at work. Fully conscious and in great pain, the poor man gave way to incoherent noises. I flew back to the house, called out the sentries, seized a bottle of brandy from the dining-room and, helped by the sentries, poured some of the spirit down the gardener's throat, until—lo and behold!—he began to revive! Two or three days later he was well again.

There! said I to myself, with a certain amount of satisfaction, I have actually been the means of saving a man's life. So original, I thought it all! A snake-bite is rather unusual in England.

Then there was a bird, about the size of a thrush, brilliant amethyst in colour, which visited the roof of my room at the Astana most afternoons about three o'clock. The bird was evidently a musician, passionately addicted to *triolets*. He would perch up there practising for half an hour at a time

beginning with A, but when he had *triolet*-ed to D he could get no further, and began again and again. Many of the English people in Sarawak were driven nearly mad when the *triolet* songsters visited their abodes, but I loved the little creature, for I looked upon him as an artist, for ever striving somehow to reach what he imagined to be perfection. Another object of interest to me was an ancient Tapang tree which I could see from my bedroom window on the edge of the jungle just by our garden. Sapless and leafless it stood, and from its high naked branches hung hundreds and hundreds of flying squirrels, looking by day like black masses of unwholesome fruit; but every evening, when the sun began to sink behind Mount Matang, the unwholesome fruit came to life, unhooked themselves from their perches, and flew over the house in an enormous black cloud, in search of fruit in gardens across the river, making little squeaking noises as they flew. It was all so strange and so pretty. If only one is granted eyes with which to see and ears with which to listen, those tropical lands are one vast theatre of changing beauty by day and night; the drawback to it all being that there are so few people who will share such pleasures with one.

Sometimes British men-of-war would find their way to Kuching. Most pleasant those visits were, for, to my mind, all the world over there are no males to be compared to those in our Queen's, or King's, Navee! The captains and officers were entertained to dinner, luncheon or tea at the Astana and appeared to enjoy themselves. Lawn tennis (then only recently introduced into Kuching), croquet, rides along our one and only road on horses lent by residents, were some of the recreations offered them. They were gay and happy interludes in our somewhat humdrum life. At every departure of such gallant gentlemen all Kuching turned out to say farewell, whilst the Rajah and myself, dignified and standing on our verandah, bade them all God-speed as they came to the Astana to say good-bye. Our very hearts seemed torn asunder as they went their way, but when, in after days, we happened to meet in England, the tight exigencies of Western civilization befogged the friendship offered and accepted in those far-off Eastern lands.

One day, too, an Italian gunboat appeared, then cruising, for some reason best known to the Italian Government, in the Malay Archipelago. Delightful individuals the officers were. My Italian not being first-rate, we all of us spoke in French. They were all music mad, and brought to us in Sarawak delightful snatches of " Mefisto- fele," Boito's opera, then new. One of the officers, a Neapolitan with a beautiful voice, first introduced me to the charming, now well-known, serenata " La Luna Immobile," when I immedi- ately became the cynosure of all those Italian eyes, accustomed, as they were, to make up to all women. Our English officials and their wives, unused to such gallantry, sat out on the verandah with the Rajah, who was hideously bored and neither could nor would join in their conversa- tion. Feeling myself a success, at the Italians' request I played through the love duet in the third Act of Gounod's " Faust." By and by my quavery soprano and the tenor of the Nea- politan were heard in impassioned unison. " Laisse moi contempler ton visage," I squawked, while he sang with love-making stage gesture! The Kuchingites looked at us, then at each other and, after saluting the Rajah, tiptoed their way downstairs to their homes ; the Rajah, left alone and very angry, walked off to bed and was seen no more. Hours went by ; the Italians and myself at the piano, having sung our way through several operas, at last realised that it was getting very late, and began to say good-night. I invented an excuse for the Rajah's departure. They did not seem to mind and, with their pretty Italian courtesy, they each kissed my hand and went back to their ship. I am ashamed to own that I had so much enjoyed the evening that I valsed round and round the room until our Chinese servants came to put out the lights! Then, pulling myself together, I went off to my room. There I found the Rajah, sitting in a rocking-chair. "Are you lost to all sense of decency," said my spouse, "that you can sing love duets under my very nose?" "But, Charlie," I said, "the fact of your very nose being present made it all so safe!" "I do not wish to argue," responded the potentate. "Your conduct to-night as Ranee of Sarawak was very undignified indeed. Even our friends left the house, and I, naturally, was obliged to go to my room." He then went off to bed and I felt just a wee bit cross. . . . Next day, however, the Italians took their leave. The Rajah was very civil in bidding them good-bye and our matrimonial differences came to an end.

CHAPTER XVI

SOME few weeks later a very delightful thing happened. The Rajah was away at the time. On the arrival of the Sarawak steamer from Singapore one morning, a letter was brought to me from Lady Jervois, the wife of the Governor, introducing a lady called Miss North, who had taken passage from that town to Kuching. Immediately on reading the letter I sent one of the Rajah's officials on board with an invitation to her to come as our guest to the Astana. The lady duly arrived. She was about forty-five years of age, tall, lean and fair; her nose was rather large, her lips were rather thin, she wore blue spectacles and was not good-looking. But the expression in her blue eyes and her charming greeting made me like her at once. "How kind of you to ask me to come," she said. "But how do you know that you will like me well enough to see me day after day?" I told her what Lady Jervois had written. "Much too favourable," said Miss North, "but how delighted I am to be here! Your country is so lovely that I am drunk with all the beauty surrounding me." Her words gave me much pleasure. I then showed her her room, bathroom and all *en suite*,

and told her that we should meet in the dining-
room for *déjeuner* at half-past twelve. It is
extraordinary how much a guest's enjoyment of
one's hospitality can do to cement a friendship.
I was pleased to see Miss North's healthy appetite,
and still more pleased when she told me the object
of her visit to the East. She was engaged on an
artistic undertaking, that of painting the more
important specimens of Eastern flowers and fruit,
and her intention was to build a gallery in Kew
Gardens for the reception of her work, which
gallery and collection she would then present to
Kew.

After luncheon Miss North was hurtlingly
energetic. With the thermometer at 80 degrees
in the shade I was longing for my siesta.
" What ! " said my friend. " Going to lie down ?
I never heard of such a thing ! And you so
young ! Oh, do come and help me install my
painting things in my room. I wonder have
they been sent up from the steamer yet."
Naturally I had recourse to Talip, who forthwith
sent to the landing-place for them. A diminutive
portmanteau evidently contained Miss North's
scanty wardrobe; but there were three easels,
different in size, two enormous cases full of completed pictures, dozens of blocks for oil paintings
and boxes and boxes full of paint brushes, char-
coals, tubes of oils; also two or three large
palettes. The boys, laden with the different
objects, came staggering up the entrance stairs

and deposited them all on the floor of Miss North's room. " Now ! " she said. " Do help me to arrange my studio." Perspiring as I was, and longing for my afternoon rest, I yet felt a certain admiration for this wonderful visitor to Kuching who had the power to hustle us all into such energetic behaviour. Just then two of our guest-rooms were empty and Miss North had chosen one with a southerly view over the river, the bazaar and the town, with its church tower emerging from a group of trees ; further off lay the forest and beyond it the horizon was bounded by a range of mountains. Miss North set about establishing herself and arranging her belongings to her liking, giving directions to the boys as to the unpacking of her numerous equipment. The white lace window curtains were speedily tied into knots of shortage, as they impeded the view ; the sun-blinds outside were pulled up to allow the sun to stream in. We both looked, and felt, extremely warm, but she did not seem to mind, as she bustled about the room in her topee, which she had not removed even for luncheon, fallen rakishly over one eye. When the easels had been placed and everything arranged to her satisfaction her room was like a furnace, and I meekly suggested going off for an hour or two's rest. " How very odd ! " she said. " Do you *always* rest like this during the day ? Such a waste of time ! But thank you so much for your kind help. Now, when do we meet

again ? " " We have tea on the verandah at
half-past four," I tentatively said, wishing to
please her and not liking to swagger too much
about being hostess. " That will do very well,"
said she, " and afterwards we can look for copy."
" Copy ? " said I, for I did not know what she
meant. " Yes," replied Miss North. " Strange
flowers I want to paint. Now, this afternoon,
after tea, we might get hold of some pitcher
plants." " What are they ? " I asked. " I never
heard of them." " What ! Why, they are the
loveliest and most extraordinary productions in
all Malaya ! We must go for a walk and look for
some." Rather ashamed of my ignorance regarding pitcher plants, I sent for one of the boat
boys, Kong Kong, who, I thought, would be
able to help us in our search. " Oh yes, Rajah
Ranee, they are very bagus (pretty). They eat
insects and living things. I know where they
grow in the jungle and can take you there."
We had hardly swallowed our tea when Miss
North, it was, gave the signal for departure.
With her topee, her very short petticoats, her
light woollen jacket and high Wellington boots
she was ready for any emergency. We got into
a boat, went a little way down the river and were
about to land when, as luck would have it, we
heard a crested bul-bul singing on the bank near
by. Miss North was beside herself with delight,
and no wonder ! for, to my mind, the song of
this bird out-rivals in beauty even the song of our

nightingale, flowing out for several minutes, rich, lovely, in exquisite tones. A musical angel, endowing human listeners with all that is most beautiful in the sounds Nature has to offer, the bul-bul's song cannot, I think, have its equal in the world. " Say nothing—say nothing ! " whispered Miss North. " At such a moment the sound of human voices would be desecration ! " I loved her for that.

When the bird's song was over, we landed on a muddy bank and followed Kong Kong into the jungle. He was very careful to guard us from a certain good-sized shrub. Rather handsome it looked, with dark green glossy leaves and terminal shoots of bright crimson. As I had seen this plant quite often, on my trips up and down the river, I knew something about it ; that the Malays consider it to be a malignant growth because of the fact that only certain persons can touch it without disastrous consequences. For instance, one person may barely brush its branches aside and immediately be attacked with fearful internal pains or total blindness lasting for a day or two, whilst others may hack off its branches, pull off its leaves, take any liberty they choose with it and escape the slightest ill effect. Moreover, the young shoots, when cooked, are excellent to eat and quite harmless to any partaker. " And what is the shrub called ? " inquired Miss North. Neither Kong Kong nor I knew ; but, anxious to give Miss North a good impression of myself as

a botanist, I stammered forth—" Well . . . Mr.
St. John, one of the Rajah's officials, has found
out that it belongs to the *Obstideminus Cani-
fornicus* family." " My dear child," said Miss
North, " you are talking great nonsense. No
such names exist in botany. Are you trying to
take me in ? " " Well ! " I thought to myself,
although she was right and I *had* been lying rather
freely, " I had only been trying to add a greater
interest to her walk that afternoon ! " At any
rate, Miss North was quite nice about it. She
only sniffed, bumped her topee more firmly on
her head, and strode on her way. After a while
we came to a footpath (natives call it a road) along
the flat marshy land leading through shrubs,
gorse, sensitive plants and what not : a line of
single, round and slippery poles, dove-tailed into
each other, excepting in places where gaps had
been left. These we had to jump over with the
greatest care, to avoid falling into the mud that
lay knee-deep some two or three feet below the
poles. Being accustomed to the gymnastics required in getting out and in the native houses
and also to the so-called country " roads," I got
on quite well, but I was much surprised at the
sight of Miss North, who made nothing of any
difficulty. With skirts kilted above her knees
and her heel-less Wellington boots, she looked as
though born for Borneo jungles, so quickly did
she get along. At length, with perspiration
streaming from every pore, induced by our

violent attempts at pole-walking, we came upon a
very bower of pitcher plants.   There they were—
all sorts, shapes, sizes and colours, wreathing themselves overhead, trailing on the ground, hanging
on various shrubs.   What a picture !   Pale green,
rose colour, dark brown, orange, in splashes over
their dark green bowls.   Above each pitcher,
large and small, hung a delicate lid, as though a
butterfly had left a tiny filmy wing over the
aperture.   Miss North had found her promised
land !   " Are you not pleased," said she, " that
I have been the means of introducing you to such
unknown but lovely leafy subjects ?   For, make
no mistake," she continued, " the pitchers are
not flowers, but an appendage to the leaves.   The
real flowers are not pretty—they are brown,
and grow in shape much like the well-known
poker plants.   The pitchers are not kindly
growths ; they are carnivorous.   And, see here,"
said Miss North, as she showed me one with a
pale green opening, ribbed and looking rather
sticky, " this opening is sweet : poor little insects
are attracted by it, fall inside and get drowned in
the water left in the cups by showers of rain."
I looked inside the pitcher and there were two or
three insects lying dead below !   " No," said
Miss North, sighing, " beautiful things are often
sent on earth to lead creatures astray !   These
poor little insects rather remind me of silly males
lured to perdition by beautiful sirens ! "   " How

true!" I said, with, I hope, becoming gravity;
but, at heart, I am afraid I had failed to visualize
either silly males or beautiful sirens. However,
the six-o'clock insect was screeching out the
time from a tree near by and it was time for us to
return. Miss North pointed out to Kong Kong
the branches of nepenthes she wanted to paint
on the morrow, impressing on him the care
required in cutting them so that little damage
should be done to the plants. Kong Kong then,
carefully carrying the nepenthes, led the way back
across the poles to the boat. It was rather pleasant
to get back to it and rest in its low comfortable
seat under the protecting roof. "How unusual,
but lovely!" said Miss North, seating herself
beside me with her high boots and undraped
knees *en évidence*. For the first time that day the
topee came off and I admired her thick fair hair,
hardly tinged with grey. "My dear," she said,
as the paddles rhythmically flopped their way
along the water whilst the perfumes of forest
lands blew across our faces on the wings of a
south-west wind, "what a divine country! How
I love it all!" And, from that moment, I did
very truly love Miss North.

Arriving home before dinner, we both enjoyed
our cold baths; and, meeting again in the dining-
room, we each did justice to Talip's menu. By
that time I was feeling somewhat exhausted, but
Miss North appeared to be fresher than ever.

Having noticed that my piano was an Erard, she confessed a great love for music and asked me to play to her. " I love Beethoven," she said ; " won't you play me one of his sonatas ? " " The Adagio of the ' Pathétique ' ? " I suggested. " Why only the Adagio ? " she asked. " I cannot bear Beethoven's sonatas in bits ! " Nothing for it, I thought, remembering, though with some annoyance, that I was hostess and bound to try to entertain my guest ! So, somehow, I got through the " Pathétique," for which she thanked me much. My hand stretched out towards her —" Good ni . . ." I began. But no !—it was not to be yet ! Smilingly, and full of good intentions, she said, " One good turn deserves another," and went to the piano. I flopped on to a chair. Presently I heard her singing Beethoven's " Adelaida," and hoped for rest after the lover's last repetition of the name. But no—still not yet ! A few more chords were struck. Then, Beethoven's " In questa tomba oscura " reached my ears with appropriate gloom. THEN—silence ! Thank God ! ! She had risen from the piano and was, at long last, saying good night ! She went her way down the verandah to her room and I went off to bed. Oh dear, what a day it had been ! And yet I was glad Miss North had come. She was an artist—she felt the beauty of our surroundings. She loved flowers and all beautiful things. So good for me to have someone to look up to. I slept well that night and dreamt that Miss North and I had speedily become good friends.

.   .   .   .   .   .

The next morning, on paying Miss North a visit in her room, I found her tranquilly disposed, seated at her easel, over which hung the nepenthes in graceful clusters. She beamed at me through her spectacles as I came in. " Oh dear ! " she said—" I am so happy," and went on dabbing the paint on her palette with a brush and smacking it here and there on a wonderful reproduction of the pale-green-and-rose model. " What would you like to do to-day ? " I asked, eager to amuse my guest. " Do ? " she answered ; " stay here and paint. This picture must be painted before the freshness of my subject wears off." I was somewhat relieved, as the results of yesterday's strenuousness had not yet worn off and I still felt rather tired. It must be remembered that our home in Kuching was situated only two degrees north of the Equator. Miss North went on talking in spite of her brushings over her picture. " One thing I like about this place is that you need no clocks. You know that at 6 a.m. the sun rises and that at 6 p.m. it sets ; and you can tell the hour by watching the sun make its way across the sky, just as you can tell the time by certain flowers that turn their faces always to it." " Yes," I said, " but I never thought about it before." " You are young," she said. " You do not *observe* enough. Begin now by observing as much as you can of what Nature teaches you and you will find a new happiness in life. Now, child," she went on, " you lunch at twelve-thirty and have tea at four-thirty. I will join you at these meals. Meantime I shall be busy with my nepenthes, and hope to finish them by tea-time; and then, if you are kind, we can wander about in your lovely garden and get fresh copy."

After tea that day we set off to wander in the garden and, by great good fortune, Miss North was greeted by the sight of roofs and trees all white, as if covered with snow. This was caused by certain orchids—which the Malays call Pigeon orchids—coming suddenly and simultaneously into bloom, as though to prepare the country for an immense bridal feast. This white festival occurs every nine weeks or so. As if at some mysterious command, all the white flowers burst into bloom at once, only, alas! to fade away by the morrow like snow under the rays of the sun. " Quite lovely ! " said Miss North. " I believe, from what I have heard, that the same phenomenon is to be found in Sumatra. Let me see—I might class it as being *Dendrobinium Cer* . . ." " A hideous name ! " I said crossly. " Try to be a bit of a Malay out here and let the pretty sight sink into our hearts as Pigeon, or Bird, orchids." " But these denominations are not scientific," said *she*. " Thank God they are not ! " said *me*. Miss North then somewhat hastily changed the conversation. " And the Rajah,

my dear, when is he coming back ? They speak
of him in Singapore with the greatest admiration,
as law-giver and ruler of his country, and the
prosperity I see here in your capital is evidence
enough that they don't exaggerate. What will
he say when he finds me here ? " " He will be
delighted," said I, " and what they say of him
in Singapore is perfectly true and right." Just
then a tiresome thought crossed my mind. " You
know," I went on, " he imagines that he is a bit
of a botanist, and when a plant or flower straggles
over the grass or path in the garden, he just lops
it off anyhow, regardless of its laws of growth,
and is often disappointed when one of them
shows symptoms of decay after such treatment."
" Oh, dear, that sounds very ruthless," said Miss
North. " But as I have had plenty of study in
botany all my life, he and I can have some good
talks together and I can put him right about
certain things." " Ye-es," said I, rather hesi-
tatingly, " but of course one must not forget that
he is a man and, like most men, thinks his way is
the right way." A week went by, Miss North
busy with her flowers and paintings and her
presence at the Astana not interfering with the
time I spent daily with my Malay friends. Our
after-tea walks or trips up the river together were
a great pleasure to me. She was always so keenly
interested in our discoveries. I remember once
when we found some marvellously coloured
brilliant turquoise crabs down on a mud-bank by

the river. They were of such a peculiarly exquisite blue that Miss North wanted to paint them, so Kong Kong caught several of them in a bucket and brought them to her next morning, when, to her great disappointment, their wonderful brilliant blue had given place to a dull yellowish green.

When my husband returned from up-country he was very pleased to find Miss North at the Astana. He was always keenly interested in any work of public importance and highly approved of her scheme to build and present a gallery of her works to Kew Gardens. One morning at breakfast Miss North said to me, "Why don't *you* try to draw and paint flowers? You can have one of my easels. Begin on a block with charcoal, and see what you can do." "How lovely!" I thought; "why not?" I knew she would be kind and try to teach me. How I enjoyed myself every morning, when my dear Miss North would dedicate an hour or two to my tuition. After a week or so I was allowed to muddle about with oil colours, and then my happiness was complete. As a matter of fact, I had learned to draw in a mild sort of way in the days of my youth and that helped me in my strivings. Also the patience of my friend was inexhaustible. At a given moment, when I fondly imagined that I had portrayed quite a decent reproduction of a hibiscus, life-size, on a wooden panel two feet by one, I gravely suggested

having it framed and hung in the drawing-room.
Miss North, while apparently approving the
somewhat untutored smearings, gently said, " I
don't know. Don't you think that darling baby
of yours would enjoy looking at it if it were hung
over a door in his nursery ? " I rather guessed
what lay at the back of her mind and, in time,
over one of the nursery doors my caricature of a
hibiscus found its place. How conceited we,
most of us, are ! Truly, young or old, a little
knowledge *is* a dangerous thing. My husband's
sincere invitation and my reiterated implorings
persuaded Miss North to remain with us for some
three months. I enjoyed every moment of her
visit, but during the last week of her stay there
was a tiny rift within the lute. And all caused
by a most gentle thing—an orchid ! My husband
had installed an orchid house in our garden and
was trying to grow a certain variety which, in his
opinion, refused to flower properly. He called
it a Vanda Lowii, but Miss North insisted that it
was a Cypripedium. . . . A few bickerings had
taken place at meals, more especially, it seemed
to me, when curry was handed round. Two or
three days before she left, Miss North told the
Rajah that she must take her easel down to the
orchid house and paint two blooms which had
just opened out. " No use," said the Rajah.
" I shall cut the whole plant down. It's the only
way of giving it a chance of flowering properly
later on." "My dear Rajah, pray believe me,

if you cut the plant down as you suggest it will certainly die. Please don't do anything so drastic!" The Rajah looked down at his plate, tugged his moustache and said nothing at first. Then, after some time—"I have lived in this country so long I think I ought to know something about orchids." "But not about transplanting them and growing them in your back garden," said Miss North, trying to be funny. The subject was then dropped.

Next morning early, when Miss North made her way to the orchid house, easel and painting materials in hand, she found the orchids which had been in flower all cut down, lying in a heap on the path below! At luncheon that day she blurted out, "Oh Rajah, how could you? the poor orchids looked as though the devil had been hacking at them." "Do you think so?" he replied. "You see, I do know a lot about gardening."

After this a certain coolness reigned between my spouse and his guest. At the dinner-party given for her entertainment on the last evening of her visit, the Rajah could not be persuaded to oblige the company with "La Donna e Mobile," nor would Miss North indulge us with her "Adelaida"—tiny incidental straws which showed the way the wind blew! However, next day, when saying good-bye to the Rajah and myself as we stood on the verandah, Miss North most charmingly thanked him for the hospitality she had enjoyed. " I shall never forget it," she said, " and shall always remember, too, your splendid government so apparent in the happiness and prosperity of all your subjects I have come across." Then I kissed Miss North and Miss North kissed me. We both felt, oh, so sad at saying good-bye. However, I met her again, in later years, in London, and our friendship lasted until she died. Bless her ! She was a dear.

CHAPTER XVII

SOME six months after Miss North's departure it became necessary for the Rajah again to organize a punitive expedition, this time against a certain less civilized tribe of Dyaks who had been causing trouble in the region north of the Batang Lupar river. So, calling upon forces of friendly Dyaks to meet him at Simanggang, he set out for that Fort, which was to be the starting-point of the expedition. My small son was in good health, an experienced and devoted Chinese ayah was his nurse and, knowing that Mrs. Mesney (the wife of the chaplain at Kuching), and Datu Isa would look after him well, I prevailed upon my husband to take me with him as far as Simanggang, where I could stay in the Fort and await his return there from up-country. It so happened that just then the " Aline," which had replaced our former yacht the " Heartsease," was in dock at Singapore, and my husband rather dreaded my undertaking the journey by river in a canoe propelled by paddles. However, as my heart was set on the trip, he gave in, and one morning we set off in the Rajah's war-canoe, roofed-in from stem to stern and paddled by fifty men. It was fitted with seats, mattresses and pillows on which one could rest comfortably or stretch with ease. When we reached the mouth of the river, owing to the state of the tide we could not proceed and had to anchor there for the night. In spite of the thick mosquito curtains the sand-flies gave us no peace and I nearly scratched myself to death. In the morning baths had to be thought of and some of the crew were sent off into the jungle to reconnoitre. A pool was found for the Rajah, and another, near by and hidden among some trees, for myself and Ima. As I always travelled in Malay costume my dressing operations were slight indeed. The day sarong and jacket being taken off, another sarong was slipped on and tied under the arms. Thus draped, I entered the pool and washed myself with a cake of soap brought for the purpose. Never having bathed before in an alfresco pool in the jungle, I was not prepared for the leeches I came in contact with in that seemingly crystal water. They fastened on my feet and legs, drew blood and did dreadful things, and dear little Ima had her work cut out tugging them off me. I hated handling the slimy things. She also suffered from them, but went on gaily pulling them off herself with her thumb and forefinger. She laughed at it all. " Tidak apa " (never mind), " they will come off in time ! " My European bathing had perhaps made me too punctilious about the strange natures of Eastern waters and forests. However, I was soon dressed and returned with Ima to the boat, where I found the Rajah, who had also bathed and dressed, looking the picture of health and comfort. " Did you find any leeches in your pool ? " I inquired, hoping he might condole with me upon my experience. " Leeches ? " he said. " Why, yes, there were a few. Were there any in yours ? They don't really hurt, you know." And there the matter ended.

Then on we went again—paddle, paddle, paddle—thank God through a quiet sea ! We arrived at Lingga that evening, spent the night under a roof and next morning had our baths in a bathroom free from leeches ! Continuing our journey, we reached Simanggang that evening at six o'clock. There we found Mr. Maxwell, the Resident, with Pangeran Matali, Abang Aing, Hadji Mohammed, all old Malay friends, waiting for us at the landing-place. Mr. Maxwell had not expected me to be of the party and appeared anxious to escort me up to the Fort at once, but as the Rajah wished to settle various matters with him immediately regarding their departure next day, Hadji Mohammed was deputed to take me up.

Having shown me the room Mr. Maxwell had vacated for the Rajah, Hadji Mohammed retired and shut the door. As I sat down on a comfortable chair to rest, I saw a pretty Dyak damsel standing by the wall. " Tabeh ! " (Hail) I said. " Manna datang ? " (Where do you come from ?) " Tuan Resident," she murmured. . . . Presently Mr. Maxwell, somewhat agitated, came to the room. " Go away quickly," he said, quite kindly, to the maiden. Then he came up to me. " Oh, Ranee, don't tell the Rajah," he said. " What do you take me for ? " said I, dignified as ever in quiet and witty repartee ! The maiden ran out and I saw her no more.

Next morning exciting things took place. Large war-boats from far and near arrived to join the Rajah's force, the chiefs and their followers looking splendid in full war-dress. A large crowd of warriors came into the Fort-room, where muskets and rifles of all descriptions, old and new, hung in the rack. The Rajah, Mr. Maxwell and the sergeants in charge of the native troops were busily examining the different firearms to decide the efficiency of their locks. Suddenly, from the middle of the Fort-room, a shot rang out ; a man was seen to put his hand to his head from where a tattered handkerchief hung down his back, while by the wall a Dyak stood shaking and trembling, an ancient blunderbuss in his hand—a relic of the Dutch occupation which, during some bygone attack by the late Rajah, had found its way into the Fort. It had come to be looked upon as harmless and played out, and yet, with its obsolete bullet and its still workable trigger, it had almost been the means of killing a man ! The Rajah severely reprimanded the Dyak for handling firearms without permission, but the Malay who had so nearly been killed was enjoying himself immensely, fluttering his torn head hand-kerchief proudly in the faces of his friends.

This, to me, highly exciting incident did not in any way retard the busy preparations going on, while men, young and middle-aged, from the Malay villages kept on pouring in, eager to enlist. The Fort-men belonging to the Fort refused to be left behind, and next morning the war-boats, each in its appointed order, set out on their progress up the river. My husband, with noted chiefs in attendance, occupied the largest war-canoe, propelled by seventy paddles. A fine sight it was to see the army afloat, my husband's canoe with its swallow-tailed flag at the stern proudly leading the procession. Such a rhythmic sound the paddles made as they scooped their way through the water! I stood on the bank with Ima, Sunok, a very old Malay Fort-man, and Fury, Mr. Maxwell's little terrier, watching until the last boat had disappeared round the bend of the river. Then, somewhat dejectedly, we four turned back and came up the hill. On reaching the Fort we sat ourselves down, I on a chair, Ima on the floor and Fury on a mat. " All the men have gone, Rajah Ranee," said Ima sadly. But no! The door opened and the elderly Hadji Mohammed appeared, followed by Sunok, bent nearly double. They were the only two men, with the exception of the cook, left to guard the Fort. " If Rajah Ranee have commands, she touch the gong and I will come to her," said

Hadji Mohammed. I thanked him gratefully and he left the room. Ima, Fury and self were once more alone. After a while I sent Ima off to the Campong to bid the Malay ladies visit me at the Fort; and in the afternoons during the Rajah's absence I was seldom in want of visitors! Of course I loved them, for were they not Malays? Tactful, courteous and anxious to relieve my solitude, it was lovely to feel that nothing but friendliness existed between us—so unlike the detestable attitude often assumed by Westerners towards the Native races. The great Rajah Brooke saw to all that and so did the white men who followed in his path.

How true it is that we have to find our happiness within ourselves. Faced with a certain amount of solitude at Simanggang Fort, I wondered how best I could while away the time. Every morning at sunrise a lovely sight met my eyes. A flash of egrets (called paddi birds by the natives) flew overhead in a dense fluttering mass of wings, naturally white, but tinged by the sun's rays into every colour of the rainbow. They flew in triangular formation, the extreme point being formed by the bird leading the flock. Regular as clockwork, the lovely creatures went their way across the river at sunrise, returning to the minute each evening as the sun set. What a wonderful sight!

Then, every fortnight, at new and full moon, for two or three days, another looked-for friend made its appearance. It is not often that civilized folk coming from perhaps smug and uninteresting places get the chance of seating themselves in a comfortable room and watching from a top window the *bore*, sighted a quarter of a mile away. Desperate, untamed, flinging great waves of spray over rocky impediments in the shallow river, it advances, undermining the banks of mud and sand ; uprooting shrubs and weeds that, thus torn off, dance along the water in its wake. Yes, I felt thankful to the Batang Lupar on account of its bore! But of course one had to find some occupation between these wonderful displays of Nature. A great friend of mine, Saripa Madjeena (a descendant of the Prophet, if you please!), brought her loom up to the Fort and began, somewhat unsuccessfully, to give me lessons in the weaving of silken and cotton fabrics, for which our Malay women are very justly famous. Alas for me! The loom was an instrument of torture. The threads were held taut in position by a wooden backboard which, to unaccustomed backs, was very painful, whilst both one's feet had to form a leverage which was very cramping to the toes. Throwing the shuttle across was also a difficult process—it often fell off my fingers. Anyhow, the Saripa's patience was infinite, and although I never became an adept at weaving, the fact of my wishing to learn—and she to teach—made us very good friends.

And so my days wore on, not at all dully.

Over three weeks having sped by, I was expecting
the return of the expedition within a few days,
when one afternoon I saw some four or five war-
canoes coming up from the mouth of the river.
The canoes, each manned by some thirty or
forty men, passed below the Fort and on to the
bazaar foreshore beyond, where they halted.
Hadji Mohammed, who had caught sight of
them, said, "They are Kayans—they are no
good—I don't much like the look of them!"
As I was always eager to welcome a new excitement, and against the Hadji's advice, I gathered
Ima, Sunok and Fury around me and marched
down the hill, my two human defenders lagging
rather half-heartedly behind me. But before I
had got half-way down there they were—about
a hundred of them—Kayans all, armed with
swords and spears, noisily making their way in a
kind of war-dance up the hill. They had
probably not seen a white woman before, but
took no particular notice of me until I stood
still and held up my hand in, I hope, a dignified
and important manner. Sunok could speak their
language but I only talked Malay. "Sunok," I
said, "ask them where they come from." "From
beyond Kanowit," was the reply vouchsafed by
a small man who had established himself at the
head of the Kayans as spokesman. "And where
are you off to?" "To join the Rajah's expedition," answered the small man. On hearing the
object of their journey and being well aware of

the danger to which unprotected villages up-country might be exposed from these undisciplined warriors without any competent leader to control their doings, I determined that at all costs they must be kept at Simanggang until the Rajah returned. " Tell them," I said to Sunok, " that I am the Rajah's wife and as such must be obeyed. The Rajah will be back in two or three days' time. Tell them they must await him here or go at once back to Kanowit. At any rate night is coming on and they cannot move, and to-morrow they are to come to the Fort, unarmed, when I shall hold a betchara (palaver) and they will learn what I want them to do." " They know we can do nothing to them and they say they intend going up-river to-morrow whatever happens." " Then tell them from me, the Rajah's wife, that if they do not obey her orders and come this evening to the Fort, to hear what further she has to say, the Rajah will make short work of them on his return."

And now—must I confess it ?—I did begin to feel a bit anxious. I was also very much annoyed to think of the possibility of my defeat. I returned to the Fort and waited. . . . The whole party of Kayans were coming up as I had commanded, *but* they were all fully armed with swords and parangs, and Hadji and Sunok, knowing our defenceless position, shook their heads with misgiving. Now it so happened that I had been in the habit of shooting at targets with a rook rifle, and this I carried about with me on my travels. A good thought came to me. Knowing how even the barrel of a rifle had power to intimidate these people, who possessed no fire-arms themselves, I marched into the room where they were assembled to meet me, my rook rifle on my shoulder. Then I sat down on a chair facing them, banging the butt end of the gun on the floor. Of course Sunok was spokesman. "See here, my friends" (I shook my rifle up and down), "here is good medicine for those who do not obey the Rajah!" They began to wobble about on the floor in apprehension. "These are his orders. You stay where you are, here in Simanggang, and await his return." Could I believe my ears? Were they daring to become truculent? Could Hadji and Sunok have rightly understood the small man declaring they would be off on the morrow whether I liked it or no? I then stood up, keeping tight hold of my rifle. "Very well," said I (of course through Sunok). "You will all be dead if you disobey my orders. Those great guns from the port-holes, which overlook the river, are all loaded and they will do their duty. And not only the guns, but my rifle also will do its duty! In a short time your disobedience will kill you all!" I shouldered my rifle and, followed by Ima and Fury, walked back to my room. The Hadji presently came to me. "But the guns are not loaded," he said, "and, in any case, we none of us can fire them."

" Never mind," said I, " they think they are and that is sufficient for our purpose." The Kayans went sullenly back to their boats, where they were obliged to remain for the night as they could not make their way with safety up-river in the dark.

I slept badly that night. But oh, joy! Just at gun-fire—5 a.m.—I heard triumphant war yells borne up to me from the river! The expedition was returning. The Rajah would be back soon! I dressed and went down to the landing-stage, where I awaited him, oddly surrounded by the troublesome Kayans! "What are you doing here?" the Rajah asked them as he stepped on shore. "Come from Kanowit to join you on the war-path." "Rather late in the day," said the Rajah. "Go back at once to where you came from." When the Hadji had told him the whole story, my husband said to me, "You did right to keep them here." That was all. And so my adventure ended in smoke. That evening Mr. Maxwell lighted the lamps for me inside my room. "My dear Ranee," said he, "the Hadji has told me all about it. You have been quite splendid!" Fond as I was of approbation, and getting so little of it, I very nearly embraced Mr. Maxwell à la française, sur les deux joues!

CHAPTER XVIII

TIME and tide, waiting for no man, rush their way along, bringing joy and sadness to all sentient beings in the world. One morning when I was sitting in the nursery at the Astana, my small boy playing on the floor beside me, my husband came into the room and put an open telegram in my hand; then quickly went out again, closing the door behind him. "George de Windt died to-day," were the words I read on the sheet. Nothing more excepting my sister-in-law's address in London. . . . For me it was an awful blow. I loved my brother George and he was devoted to me. My brother Harry had left Sarawak some time ago and I was therefore all alone, to get over the shock as best I could. My little boy, seeing me cry, rubbed his darling head against my knee. I got up and went off into the garden and sat myself down on a seat overlooking the river, where I remained until the late afternoon. I do not imagine that the Rajah even inquired into my absence from breakfast, as he was really quite incapable of showing sympathy or feeling about anything that did not touch Sarawak. After all, a leopard cannot change its spots, and the Rajah could not help being bored by any manifestations of sorrow. I realized all this and, knowing that life had to go on as usual, I at last pulled myself together late in the afternoon, went indoors and joined him at dinner that evening. During the meal my brother's name was never mentioned by either of us. Afterwards I went into the nursery. My little boy was awake and flung his arms round my neck, while his Chinese ayah (who had been a Mission girl in Bishop MacDougall's time) put her arm round me and said, "Don't cry, Rajah Ranee; your brother is with God, waiting for you up there," and she pointed to the ceiling. Sympathy is a great consolation, wherever found, and I was grateful to her. I slept with my little son that night and felt comforted by his nearness and love. Next morning I was able to take breakfast with my husband, and later, after tea, to go with him for a row on the river.

A year or so later another baby appeared on the scene, destined, like his brother, to grow to manhood and become, with him, the pride and glory of his mother's heart. Datu Isa and my devoted Malay women friends, always in attendance as usual, became almost hysterical with delight, the more so because the new baby had been born in Sarawak.

The Rajah once more became active on the subject of procuring a wet nurse for his new son. "My dear Rajah," said the doctor, "where am I to find one?" However, a Chinese woman who,

like our ayah, had been brought up in the
Mission by Mrs. MacDougall, was found, and it
was arranged that her baby should be fed on
goat's milk so that she should be able to feed
the Rajah's son, which she regarded as a great
honour. The young woman, christened Fanny
years before by the Bishop, was generally known
as Penny, for the Chinese cannot pronounce an
F, and was a charming creature; her baju and
sarong spotless and her lovely hair, dressed in
pretty shining coils of darkness, was kept neat
and tidy by golden-headed hairpins. The doctor
was well pleased, so was the Rajah, so was I.
The child took to his nurse with hungry satisfaction and all went well. The English ladies
in Kuching, however, were rather perturbed.
" Fancy an English baby being fed by a Chinese ! "
said they. " Surely goat's milk would have been
preferable. The child might imbibe Chinese
oddities being subjected to such a diet ! " In this
way during calls and parties they were rather
tiresome. Luckily I have always cared little for
public opinion and was not small-minded. Knowing my dear Penny well and the devotion she bore
to my child, I allowed them to chatter away and,
when they became too much of a bore, let drop
the well-known saying, " Are we not all the
children of one Father ? " Inadequate as an
argument, I admit, but it put an end to their
interference.

A short time after Penny was installed, the

English nurse, Miss Clements, arrived from England. She took to Sarawak at once, loved my children and the country and took a great fancy to Penny, giving it as her firm conviction that the little boy was as healthy as could be wished under her motherly care.

And now I began to ail somewhat seriously. The malaria which tries so many Europeans in the tropics (although in Sarawak it is never of a virulent kind) took hold of me in a most unpleasant way. Unlike the more common symptoms usually experienced by English people —ague, high temperature and violent perspiration—my symptoms, which I shared with many of the Malays, were much more painful and shattering to the nerves. The Malays called the illness " ulu ati," and it bears a striking resemblance to that painful and deadly disease, angina pectoris. It smacks you down suddenly and you are in an instant bent double and gasping for breath. If you attempt to sit up you feel as though knives were hacking at you under your shoulder-blades and you have to remain propped up with pillows, maybe for hours, and with pillows under your chin, imagining that each moment may be your last. The curious feature of these attacks is that your pulse remains normal and the heart-beats undisturbed. Sudden as its seizures are, just as sudden is the relief, for in one second the attack will pass off and all pain and discomfort vanish. The Malays all thought that malaria was the underlying cause of my frequent sufferings, but our doctor appeared nonplussed by my symptoms and never, with any of his medicine, did he do me the slightest good. "No cause for alarm," said he to my husband. "Heart and pulse are normal. Maybe it might have something to do with hysteria." Hysteria!—that blessed refuge of somewhat unskilful doctors who find themselves unable to diagnose a disease! My English nurse, becoming alarmed, and disagreeing with our doctor's opinion that there was nothing to worry about, insisted on weighing me at frequent intervals, when it was found that I was rapidly losing weight. "Weight has nothing whatever to do with health," pronounced the doctor, in spite of the fact that my attacks were of almost daily occurrence. All and sundry were beginning to get rather bored by my uninteresting and undiagnosable illness. "Your old chest again!" the Rajah would say quite cheerfully, as he prepared for his ride in the late afternoon, while I would be lying gasping for all I was worth. At that hour, too, the children, the nurse and Penny all had to take their daily exercise, so it happened that I would often be left quite alone for an hour or two in my mosquito house.

One day, my side of the Astana being deserted, I was in bed, feeling very sorry for myself, when the door of my mosquito house was opened by a very old Chinaman, one of the water-bearers. In his hand he held a glass filled with a pale greenish liquid. This he presented to me asking me to drink it. " Sakit benar (very ill), Rajah Ranee," he said. " I know what it is. Drink my obat (medicine)—it will do you good." Weak and gasping, I drank off the green liquid. " Now wait," said my new and original medico ; " I will make you quite well." He left the room and returned in a few minutes with a long wooden baignoire from my bathroom, which he proceeded to fill with hot water. He then came to me (I was feeling so ill that I hardly knew what was going on), lifted me out of bed and, then and there, plunged me, nightgown and all, into the bath, where I lay up to the chin in very hot water. All of a sudden, whether owing to the Chinaman's medicine and hot bath I know not, my breathing became normal again and the pains vanished, but I was too weak to get out of the bath. However, tactful, thoughtful and kind, the old man handed me a sheet and I just managed to stand up and wrap it around me, letting the wet nightgown drop. He then carried me back to bed, heaped blankets over me and left the room. I soon dozed off into a sound sleep, and when the Rajah returned from his ride, the children and the nurses from their walk and the doctor arrived to pay his visit, they were all delighted with my improved condition. " Hysteria, you think it ? " said the Rajah. " All hysteria," said the doctor, and they left it at that.

Oddly enough the attacks did not return, but

I had become so thin and weak and felt so ill that I told the Rajah I should die, I thought, if I did not get a change to England. I must say he acquiesced at once and in a month's time we shipped on a P. and O. liner at Singapore on our way home. By that time Bertram was two years old and Penny was no longer required. He and his brother were fine little fellows, quite able to face the sea journey. As for me, goodness knows how it all happened, but by the time we reached Point de Galle I was almost restored to health and gaining strength every day. By the way, like two conspirators, the old Chinaman and I never alluded to his medical remedies, administered behind the doctor's back. He had been successful where our doctor had failed. I found out afterwards that the green liquid which I had swallowed was composed of monkeys' gall-stones, powdered and diluted with water. I wonder whether such ingredients are ever used in European medicines!

We all remained in the best of health during the voyage and our few days' stay in London. We were disappointed at not being able to rent Rodbourne again that winter as Sir Hungerford Pollen was living there himself, but we were lucky in getting Cole Park, which was only about a mile distant, and we established ourselves there. So we were once more in the midst of our delightful friends in Wiltshire, my dear Pollens close at hand and my husband getting plenty of hunting.

And yet, for me happiness was not complete. Another addition to our family was expected early that winter and my son Harry was born at Cole Park in November. I really began to wonder whether my rabbit-like propensities would ever cease. This event rather spoiled my holiday, but grumbling only makes matters worse and it is better, like the gentle roseau in La Fontaine's fable, to bend to the inevitable instead of being broken by it as was the sturdy oak which tried to resist the storm. Our nurse, Clements, was in her element; happiness simply oozed from her while she held the new baby in her arms, but my two other little sons resented an unknown in their midst and threw wet sponges at him as he lay sleeping in his cot if his nurse happened to be looking the other way.

Now that all inconveniences regarding his arrival had come to an end I dearly loved my new little boy. A very fine baby he was! Congratulations poured in on us. Dear Katey Pollen was his godmother and Sir Harry Keppel, that marvellous man who had sailed as conqueror over many seas, came to Cole Park to stand as his god-father at the font, the baby receiving the names of Harry Keppel, and very proud he was of them in later years. I cannot help saying here a word or two of my admiration for that tiny statured but very great man. About five feet high, he barely reached my shoulder. So great were my affection and admiration for him that one day at Cole

Park, being a creature of unrestrained impulses, I flew at him as he stood by a window, knelt before him and kissed his hand. " Oh, Sir Harry," I said, " you were a friend of the great Rajah's and helped him to sweep away the pirates and to make Sarawak what it now is ! " " My dear," he said, " you mustn't do that." And, kicking a footstool near to my feet, he stood on it and kissed me. " You are young and I am old," he went on, " but thank you all the same." Bless him ! Sir Harry Keppel was admired by all as a hero and beloved by everyone as a friend.

The christening went off just as my husband would have wished. The Rajah ordered out the coach and the somewhat unruly four-in-hand (luckily for me I had not recovered sufficiently to undertake the drive !), the innocent baby and his nurse were stuffed inside, Katey Pollen was placed on the box seat and Sir Harry, my brother Harry and one or two other men were seated outside. The team ran away, in a manner of speaking, all along the drive—about a mile in length—and tore with renewed frenzy up the hill to Rodbourne Church. The return from the church was even more full of peril, as the hill was a steep one and the brakes were smoking from the tension which had to be applied to them. The party, however, arrived back unscathed, steam pouring from the horses' flanks. " Touch and go, that, Admiral ! " said my husband. " Indeed yes ! " said Sir Harry. " How about the baby inside ? " Of a certainty, both the Rajah and his friend enjoyed somewhat rollicking experiences !

As our holiday in England drew to a close, that everlasting problem of so many English wives whose husbands' avocations happen to be on the other side of the world began to worry me. My duty then was to return to Sarawak with my husband as long as the three boys were young enough to thrive under trustworthy, although not a mother's, care at home. A tropical country is, of course, not good for young children and we were determined to run no risks. We were very fortunate in being able to persuade Mrs. Nicolets, a widowed sister of the Rajah's, to look after our children. She and I were very good friends and I knew that in her care, and Clements', they would be safe and happy. Sometimes I wondered, half in sadness, half in joke, whether, had I been forewarned of the requirements which would be heaped upon me by my husband, I should have been so ready to skip with him half across the world and become " his queen " !

But, after all, who has ever attained complete happiness in this life ? Neither, maybe, would it be good for one. Hurtlings here and there make one better understand the problems of life. At any rate, when I left my three beloved boys that dismal morning in London and kissed their darling rosy sticky faces (they were just finishing their bread and honey at the end of breakfast)

I felt miserable indeed. To save me the longer
sea journey my husband had decided to board the
Messageries Maritimes steamer at Genoa. We
stayed a night at Venice on our way—that
romantic, gondola-haunted spot, which impressed
me not one bit, so sad I was for those I had left
behind. I was glad when we got to Genoa and
began our voyage. The captain of the steamer
was a charming, gallant individual. An important French official in the Colonial Service was on
board, with his wife, on their way to Cochin
China. We sat together at the captain's table
and the French lady took a dislike to me, as she
detested the English. One day the lady led the
conversation to the subject of ankles, thick and
thin. " I never saw an Englishwoman," said she,
rather rudely, " whose ankles could in any way
compare with those of my countrywomen ! "
" Oh, Madame," replied the captain, with a leer
and a wink in my direction. " J'ai pu, ici à bord,
constater le contraire ! " " Impertinent fellow ! "
muttered the Rajah, while the French lady
coughed behind her handkerchief ; her husband
remained silent and the captain and I exchanged
smiles of friendliness until the meal was over.
The voyage was quite pleasant and uneventful and
when Kuching was reached we resumed our life
as of old, the Rajah busy with affairs of government and I surrounded by my dear Malay
friends who were eager for news about my three
boys in England.

Then, as time went on, my health again began to give way. The same tiresome attacks of what our doctor described as " hysteria ! " made my life a burden, and about two years later, so ill had I become that the Rajah thought it better I should return to England for some years' stay, where he could rejoin me for a time at no very distant date. I could then be with my children and look after them.

And now followed a period when I felt helpless indeed. As all my husband's thoughts were entirely centred on Sarawak and its welfare, it is really not surprising that he was completely ignorant regarding the financial requirements of family home life in England. His wife and children belonged to him and in no circumstances were they to interfere with, or encroach upon, the prosperity of Sarawak. However, monetary arrangements had to be gone into and I naturally sympathized with his wish that the Sarawak treasury should not be depleted on my account. I looked forward to making a home with my children, but I realized how greatly my utter ignorance of business matters would be against me (never having had, since my marriage, a cent to spend of my own). Monetary troubles began to loom tragically on my horizon. " Let us get a pencil, Charlie," said I, " and put expenses down. Now I have £800 a year of my own, left me by my mother; that will help a bit with the annuity Sarawak can afford me."

" Nonsense," said my husband, " what's yours is mine." " Well then, Charlie," said I, " will you ask your brother or sister in England to help me with the necessary arrangements, as it all frightens me very much ? " " Nonsense," he said again, " you can easily find out things for yourself. And, mind you, I won't have my family interfering in my private affairs ! I will give you £2000 a year—a most ample allowance, and you must manage to keep within that limit."

When my husband said good-bye to me on board the steamer at Singapore, he gave me six five-pound notes, which were deducted from my first month's allowance. This was to pay for my journey from Marseilles to London and to cover incidental expenses on the homeward journey. Oh dear ! When the ship moved off and I locked the money up in my cabin I felt afraid, for the first time in my life, at the approaching intricacies of pounds, shillings and pence. My apprehensions were much greater than they had ever been when I was called upon to face the most bloodthirsty of Dyak head-hunters.

After all, in writing one's reminiscences it behoves one to tell the truth—even against oneself. I had suffered so much during my married life in never being able to give presents here and there or to help people I met on my way, that whilst on board I could not resist helping some of the poverty-stricken passengers travelling in the steerage, whom I used to see in their wretched discomfort in my peregrinations round the ship, thus depleting very considerably the precious thirty pounds. Silly, of course, but then I *was* silly and totally unfit to cope with the business side of affairs.

When we arrived at Suez a very interesting personage came on board—the Prince Héréditaire de Monaco. We made good friends, seated side by side at meals with the captain. Prince Albert was much interested in Sarawak and had read all about our first Rajah's doings out there—" one of the great romances of the world," he said; and he was never tired of asking me about our dear people, confessing even to a certain sympathy with the head-taking Dyaks, laughingly saying that he wished he might follow their example and rid the world of certain European heads he had in mind ! My friendship with Prince Albert ripened into deep affection on both sides, and when, later, having succeeded to the Principality, he married Alice, Duchesse de Richelieu, I counted them both amongst my greatest friends in the world.

Arrived in London I flew to my sister-in-law's house, situated in Russell Road—" at the back of beyond," said my brother Harry and some friends who were bored by the long drive out to West Kensington, to what they casually described as the suburbs ! There I found my precious trio—my second boy, Bertram, so excited over my arrival that he was promptly sick after tea.

My sister-in-law, in her wonderful generosity, was quite ready to let me live with her until the time when her brother should join me later, and I was ready to jump at the suggestion, for what cared I how people sniffed at the Russell Road as long as I had my precious ones under my wing! My brother and my friends, however, would not hear of such an arrangement. " Think of your position as Ranee," they said. " It would do your country a lot of harm and the Rajah would not like it." " All very well," I thought, " but you none of you know my monetary dilemmas ! " My brother Harry, anxious to see that I was established in a " suitable " neighbourhood, called for me next day in a hansom and we went from agent to agent, finally deciding on a quite nice, furnished, house in Cornwall Gardens, large enough for us all, including the Rajah when he should return. The rent was £400 per annum. " Oh, Harry," said I in agony, " how much does that mean a week ? " " Quite a small sum," said he, " but what does that matter to you ? Why worry ? " " Of course not," I agreed ; but I spent a couple of hours that evening with my tongue out, calculating, pencil in hand, the hole that this sum would make in my allowance !

Harry took the business of buying plate, linen, glass and crockery off my hands. That came to over £300. A man-servant, a cook, my own maid, a housemaid and a kitchenmaid were then engaged. Their estimated wages, added to dear

Clements' £40 a year, made my heart sink. Oh
dear, thought I, why couldn't I go alone with
Clements and perhaps one maid to a cottage in
the country and live far from the madding crowd
and all expense! Another item of expenditure
somewhat necessary to me in London (for I had
never been without some means of conveyance)
was a modest one-horse brougham, but the cost
of hiring it (£6 10s. per week) was an outlay not
to be thought of. Never had I passed such
anxious moments, more especially as everyone
seemed to imagine that I was *rich*, and of course
I could not "let down" my poor dear or our
beloved Sarawak. My brother Harry, not knowing the stringent need for economy, had spent
much more than I could afford on his purchases
for me, and it was all very difficult. But I had
to face matters squarely. My mother had left
me some very fine diamonds and pearls and, much
against my will, I was obliged to dispose of several
pieces of jewellery in order to make good the
deficit in my bank account. When this had been
done I felt very much relieved in mind and was
able to enjoy the society of many friends and
relatives who were constantly asking me to dinner-
parties and entertainments.

My position as the Rajah's wife frequently
occasioned inquiries from my Society friends.
They acknowledged quite frankly that they did
not know what to do about me regarding
my precedence at dinner-parties. The Lord

Chamberlain was even referred to on the subject. "Oh yes," said he, "I believe her husband does call himself Rajah. Better treat her as Mrs. Brooke; I think that will be all right." About this time I became acquainted with Sir Thomas and Lady Brassey, who knew something about Sarawak. Lady Brassey invited me to dinner and treated me to a red carpet, at which I was not surprised, and I walked up it with great confidence. After all, was not my husband an independent sovereign as far as the internal policy of his country was concerned, although, Sarawak being under British protection, its foreign policy was controlled by Britain. However, none of my other friends knew much about it all and their fussings and worryings about according to me my precedence at their parties did not bother me in the least. It was quite enough for me that in inviting me to their houses they meant to be kind and hospitable, but I could not help at times being amused by their perpetual " you *are's* " and " you are *not's*."

A year or two went by. My house in Cornwall Gardens proved a great success. My three sons had now reached an age when they required a governess and I was fortunate enough to induce Mrs. Flood, a sister of the famous and much-admired Lady Tree, to spend some hours daily with my three bairns. Mrs. Flood proved to be a wonderful guide to youth and managed to interest the children in everything needful to develop them into intelligent and kindly human beings. They became everything that a mother's heart could wish, and I fully realize that Mrs. Flood's early tuition was largely responsible for the wonderful manly qualities they developed in later years.

But I must confess that the future education of my sons presented a difficulty to me. The Rajah would never listen when I spoke to him on the subject, and so unknowing was he in the matter of suitable schools that he gravely suggested in one of his letters that they should be sent to the Blue Coat School. Most fortunate for me it was that I had met at the house of Lady Londonderry a gentleman well known in the Foreign Office, Sir Clement Hill, a very serious-minded delightful man. He it was advised me to put their names down for Eton and also for Harrow at very good houses in both schools, and he kindly undertook this task for me. I duly acquainted my husband with this fact by letter, and he seemed perfectly satisfied and ready to decide on either Eton or Harrow whenever our sons should be old enough for school. Mrs. Trotter, a Wiltshire friend, recommended a preparatory school for them in Devon to which I sent them, and they made friendships there which have lasted them till their later years. Then when the time came and I was awaiting my husband's decision as to whether they should go to Eton or to Harrow, he suddenly informed me that they must be sent to *Winchester*, where no preliminaries of any sort had been made for their reception. It was all very perplexing and annoying and the difficulties appeared to me to be gigantic! I knew not what to do. A friend of mine, however, Mr. Harry Higgins, known by everyone in London and greatly beloved by all, was a great help to me in this matter and he kindly managed to get them taken into the house of a master he knew at Winchester. Luckily their stay there was successful on the whole, although the climate of that town, being relaxing, did not agree with either of them. Then Bertram had a serious accident at football. He was violently kicked in the back, and this resulted in severe injuries to the spine, so that he was laid up for four years of his young life. Meanwhile, after Vyner had spent some years at Winchester, the Rajah decided, and very rightly, that it was time for him to visit Sarawak and be introduced to his people and his country before going up to his University. Vyner, accordingly, started off with a tutor, a young man named Fiennes, who had been recommended by Mr. Harry Higgins and who became a great friend and proved a satisfactory mentor. After staying out there for some months Vyner returned to England in order to go to Cambridge, to Magdalene College.

During my life in London I was lucky enough to become surrounded by the most delightful friends. I went to Paris too, now and then, taking Bertram with me by doctor's orders, as change and quiet amusement were essential to his recovery. I took rooms at the Hôtel d'Albe, at the top of the Champs Élysees, a healthy spot, especially at the season of our visit, which was in April. By this time the Prince de Monaco had married the Duchesse de Richelieu. Her two charming children, Armand, then Duc de Richelieu, and his sister Odille, were delightful friends for Bertram and they spent many happy hours together. The Princesse and I became intimate friends. The Princesse Mathilde was a great friend of Alice de Monaco's. She was first cousin to Napoleon III and had lived in Paris during his reign. When Sédan and the downfall of the Empire occurred, Princesse Mathilde, being a member of the Imperial family, had to leave France. She remained in exile for some years, after which Thiers, then President of the Republic, recognizing her popularity with whatever government held sway in France, allowed her to return to Paris.

When Princesse Mathilde heard from the Princesse de Monaco that I was in Paris I received an invitation to her house in the Rue de Berry. The Princesse received most evenings, and on one occasion the Monacos and I, having dined, hied ourselves to her door. On entering the reception room at the end of which our hostess sat enthroned, surrounded by her guests, Princesse Mathilde beckoned to me and invited me to a seat beside her on her right. " Now," she said, looking straight at me and smiling, " Causons ! " I sat admiring her, she was so natural, so spontaneous ; it was a joy to be with her. In her youth she had been beautiful, but at that time (in the 'nineties of last century) she appeared to me to look much the same as many other dowagers of about sixty look all the world over. When she spoke, however, her features were lit up by flashing and responsive eyes ablaze with interest, understanding, kindness and humour. She was dressed simply and on the aged side, and some black lace was draped over her thick dark hair which was turning grey. " And your father and mother were English," she said, " but you have des gouttes de sang français in your veins." " Oh yes, Altesse," I said, " and those drops make me to my mind entirely French, heart and soul. I look upon France as my native land." " Très bien," she answered, approvingly, "and you talk French as well as we do. But tell me," she went on, " you have a country all your own. Your husband is a king in a land aux antipodes ? " " Yes, that is so," I replied. " And Alice tells me you are happy there. But it must be trying to live in so icy cold a land ! " " Icy cold ! " said I. " Oh yes, I know," she answered. " It is Kamtchatka, near the Arctic regions, where you must be all the time wrapped up in furs ! " The Prince de Monaco coming up to talk to her at that moment, I left it at that. After all, why worry about the matter? She had evidently received a garbled version of Sarawak from Alice de Monaco and had a very confused idea about my having a country of mine own. At any rate the evening was a delightful one.

I slipped out of the chair beside the Princesse and went to talk to Pierre Loti, whom I had already met frequently at the Monacos' house. We always got on very well. His beautiful books, written during his Eastern travels, enchanted me, nor could I forget that he was one of the few Europeans who had, years before, when a midshipman in a French man-of-war, visited Easter Island and written about it. A bond of union that I had with this great writer-poet was his sympathy with the natives in the Eastern countries he had visited. I admired his wide-mindedness with regard to coloured races and shared his intolerance of the English and European standards concerning Eastern peoples. Then he loved the Turks—the Old Turks—and so did I. A short time before he died he sent me one of his last books, *La Turquie Agonisante*, and I cherish it as a remembrance of our friendship. Another thing makes me very proud. He dedicated one of his charming sketches to me— " L'Impératrice Printemps " in his book *Japonneries d'Automne*. Appreciating him and admiring him as I did, nothing could have given me greater pleasure.

At the Princesse de Monaco's house one was

privileged to meet other great French writers—
Bourget, Maupassant, Ganderax, Hugues Le
Roux and many others. They were all kind and
nice to me, firstly because I was a great friend of
their hostess, and secondly because of the trickling
of French blood in my veins and the fact that I
much preferred talking in French to talking in
English. Maupassant liked me because I happened to say, at one of the Princesse's dinner-
parties, that some years previously, while in
Sarawak, I had come across a saying of his in
La Revue de Paris, an exquisite line which I had
carried about in my heart ever since. " But,
Madame," they said, " Maupassant was never
known to write anything in the *Revue de Paris*."
" But yes, Messieurs," I insisted, " he did."
(All this time Maupassant remained silent.) " It
was during a journey he made to Sicily, when he
was walking on the island and suddenly came on a
grove of orange blossoms in full flower. The
scent was so delicious that he describes it as ' une
sensation de bien-être qui est presque du bon-
heur ! ' " I looked at Maupassant, who rose from
the table and kissed my hand. " C'est parfaite-
ment vrai ! " he said, " et c'est à Borneo que j'ai
trouvé votre cœur !—à Borneo ! " I thought
him perfectly charming.

At another of the Princesse's delightful dinner-
parties a somewhat queer incident occurred. One
of the younger *littérateurs* present, hearing two
of the guests talking of the suicide of a Russian

lady who had drowned herself the previous
Sunday in one of the Italian lakes—supposedly
pour cause d'amour!—suddenly groaned out
" Pour moi—pour moi! " and fell from his chair
to the floor.   All present, including the Princesse,
whilst inwardly rather pleased, pitied the fallen
one from their hearts.   Dinner had barely reached
the first entrée but all came to a stop.   " Ce pauvre
garçon," they said.   " Voyons, remettez-vous! "
" Impossible! " he groaned as he sat himself up
on the floor.   " Ah, Madame," he said, turning
to me, " un peu de Wagner au salon . . ."
" C'est çà," cried out all the other guests, " jouez
lui du Wagner—ça le remettra! "   Nothing for
it!   So I rose and he followed me into the drawing-room, where I played him the love duet from
" Tristan."   " Madame, ça me fait du bien! "
he said, then begged for bits out of " Die Wal-
küre."   When I had finished and he had grown
calm, we returned to the dining-room, where
ices were being handed round!   The ravaged
one murmured, " Ah, les tragédies nous ôtent
l'appétit! "   But as for me, I was very hungry
and I had missed all my dinner!   However, I
consoled myself by thinking that my Wagner
medicine had done him good, for its listener
appeared gay and light-hearted for the rest of the
evening !

Another French writer, although not quite so
sérieux as the rest, was Hugues Le Roux.   We
had many interests in common.   Maybe the

years I had spent among my so-called uncivilized Dyaks had given me a taste for trying to understand the idiosyncrasies of all sorts and conditions of men. Through Le Roux I heard of the existence of a certain haunt of thieves, then called the Château Rouge, where—although to some extent supervised by the police—thieves and supposed assassins of all ages and degrees of villainy congregated most evenings from about eight o'clock until two in the morning. Its attic—a long low chamber under the eaves—was invariably filled with homeless beings who were allowed to seek shelter and rest there until that hour, when they were obliged to quit the premises. Le Roux asked me if I would like to visit the place. " Don't tell the Princesse," he said, " she would not approve." I at once arranged a rendezvous for the very next evening. " Dress yourself as a femme du peuple," he said, " and put a large cloak over your dress." I was delighted. The next morning I went off to the Bon Marché, bought myself a suitable dress of blue cotton, a red apron dotted over with white spots, white stockings and thick land shoes and a handkerchief, nondescript in colour, to tie over my head. I called in a fiacre for Le Roux at his house and he greatly approved my appearance. Oh dear, how I enjoyed myself! We dined at a humble estaminet near by—a fricot and omelette au rhum, not at all bad—and after eight o'clock we took our way on foot to the Château Rouge. I was very much interested in the building, which was originally erected by Henri IV's orders for Gabrielle d'Estrées. Its walls, dark and be-grimed, yet showed here and there frescoes of what were, I believe, hunting scenes. It stood on the other side of the Seine, not far from Notre Dame, but I have been told that it has since been pulled down. In answer to my companion's knock, the door was first of all pulled only slightly ajar, when Le Roux spoke one or two words which were, I think, pass-words. Then the door was opened wider and we were admitted. On entering we found ourselves in the midst of an original and curious-looking company of men and women of all ages. The men in casquettes, round hats or bare-headed; clean-shaven, bearded or with moustaches waxed or pendant—some fairly clean and neat, others dirty and unkempt. I noticed that they nearly all wore red ties—a sort of joke among them that the guillotine might one day require them! The women were also a strange assortment—some of them quite young and pretty, others hag-like and dressed in rags. As Le Roux and I went in all talk stopped and they stared at me, a stranger in their midst. A three-legged stool was un-tenanted near a pretty girl who sat holding a dachshund on her lap. I went and sat down beside her, still stared at by the company, who kept nudging each other and whispering. Deter-mined to try my best in my present surroundings,

I turned to the pretty girl and said, " Ah, citoyenne, quel joli petit chien vous avex là." " N'est-ce-pas ? citoyenne, je l'aimes beaucoup, cette petite bête." " Viens, mon tou-tou, comme tu es gentil," said I. She smiled at me ; I was getting along very well. The dog laid his head on my lap and began to lick my hand—a diplomatic gesture on his part !—and his owner began to talk to me at once. Just then a most awful-looking ruffian—red-tied, of course—nudged Le Roux and, indicating me, said, " Présentez moi." " Anastasie," said Le Roux, addressing me, " Anastasie, this is Boucher." Boucher then shook " Anastasie " by the hand very heartily indeed, saying at the same time to Le Roux, " Mes compliments, mon cher, elle est *très* bien ! " Rather embarrassing for me, but after all, " When in Rome . . ." etc. ! My new acquaintance had brought his guitar with him. " Voyons, citoyenne, vous aimez la musique ? " " Oh oui," I answered, " et beaucoup ! " " Alors, je vais vous chanter quelque chose." At this offer Le Roux looked somewhat perturbed and said, " If he sings anything too improper we must get up and go away. You must pretend you are having an *étourdissement*." But no reason at all for alarm. The bandit-looking individual tuned up his instrument and sang—of all things ! " Rappelle—toi ? " by de Musset, to one of Mozart's well-known tunes. After which he blew me a kiss from out of his two fingers. " Charmant !

citoyen," I said. "Merci!" And then I thought the time had come for a small amount of jollification in my corner of the room. At my request Le Roux managed to get hold of about two dozen glasses, filled with some horrible but very strong liquid with plums lying at the bottom. Le Roux and I took one each and trinquéed with the men and women surrounding us. "A la santé du Château Rouge!" I cried out, lifting my glass above my head. The young girl by me echoed my toast and drained her glass, regretting that her tou-tou could not join in! I am not really fond of low company, but I did enjoy myself that night, and Le Roux, accompanying me as far as my hotel, informed me that we had been a great success. I forgot to say that we took a tender farewell of my drinking friends and much looked forward to another meeting. What happened to them all, I wonder. . . . Poor dears, they were all so pleasant to me. Surely circumstances and not their own misdeeds had degraded them to where they had fallen! And, who knows, some of them may by now have risen to heights undreamed of in a kinder and more understanding world!

CHAPTER XIX

SHORTLY after my return to London the Rajah paid one of his frequent visits to England, and through him I came upon a lovely individual who was destined to remain my friend throughout his life—the Reverend Stopford Brooke. His name is well known throughout the Empire. Originally belonging to the Church of England, he was for some years Chaplain in Berlin to Her Imperial Highness the Crown Princess of Prussia (daughter of Queen Victoria). He married a Miss Beaumont, sister to the first Lord Allendale. One son and six daughters were born to the couple, but Mrs. Stopford Brooke dying whilst the daughters were still children, their Aunt Cecilia, their father's sister, kept house for him and watched over their youth. After some time Stopford Brooke left the Church of England and adopted the Unitarian form of belief; but in whatever Church he ministered, all will agree that his sermons and addresses were magnificent. He was a born orator. In literature, also, he stood among the highest. Some of his works had reached me in Sarawak and I had spent many an hour in the enjoyment of the beautiful English that flowed through his pages. Oddly enough, somehow, somewhere, my husband and Stopford Brooke had become acquainted, Stopford Brooke being an ardent admirer of the great Rajah's work and also of the way in which my husband, his successor, carried it on. But the two men never became friends in the ordinary sense of the word, for, as I have already stated, my spouse avoided all ties of that sort which were not in Sarawak. And yet, one day, much to my surprise, the Rajah actually requested me to write and invite him to dinner. For my part, I was overjoyed, and being always ready to pounce on the possessors of any virtues admired by me in literature or any of the arts, I meant this time to pounce for all I was worth. Needless to say, the invitation was speedily sent out and, to my joy, it was accepted by return of post. My husband, for once, took great interest in the party, but we did not agree on the subject of those who were to be invited to meet the great man. Among others I suggested Sir Harry Keppel and Miss Burdett Coutts, who had both been such wonderful friends to Sarawak and the first Rajah, but my husband waved them aside. " Clergymen," he said, " always prefer a quiet homely party; moreover," said he, " it will be necessary to ask him to say grace—a most tiresome fashion handed down since that absurd Reformation ! "

I thought it best to let him have his own way. Whereupon he drew up a list of the guests he imagined best suited to meet with his Reverend-ship. Here they are. Mrs. Nicolets, his sister, a great dear who hardly ever spoke, one or two Sarawak officials who were never known to give tongue in the presence of the Rajah, a gentleman from the Borneo Company, who most probably had never heard of Stopford Brooke's existence, and a deaf old lady (I quite forget her name) who had been generous to the Sarawak S.P.G. mission many years before. I had my doubts about the amount of liveliness which would be produced on the occasion by the presence of such very reputable and home-loving folk, but it could not be helped—Stopford Brooke was coming to our house and that was enough for me !

On the evening of the dinner-party all arrived punctually to the minute *except* Stopford Brooke, who came five minutes late. The assembled ones looked at the clock and coughed slightly disapproving sounds of belatedness on the part of the clergyman, mingled with apprehensions of non-arrival ! Then, at last, in he came, bringing with him a gust of something healthy, joyous and kindly to all. A man of the world in manner, with good-fellowship and courtly feeling underlying it all. He was very good-looking too, radiating a good-natured sense of humour in all he said and did. Then we went down to dinner and I squeezed his arm tight, " How lovely of you to come," I said, and oh, joy ! my arm was squeezed back again ! The grace went off quite nicely at my husband's invitation. Then soup,

fish, entrées came in and went their way. Hardly
a word was spoken. Oh dear, it was very dull.
Suddenly, apparently apropos of nothing, the
old lady, the generous one towards the mission,
poked a speaking tube at the Rajah, who nearly
jumped off his chair. " Fine weather for the
time of year, Rajah." " Fine weather," he
replied. " Oh yes, certainly,"—and dropped the
holder. I piped out remarks as best I could to
the great man, who sat next me at dinner, but in
spite of our efforts, for he came gallantly to the
rescue, hilarity in its broadest sense was not
particularly noticeable that evening ! I managed
to throw out in stage whispers that I had read his
Beowulf and a volume of his sermons, that I loved
all he wrote, etc., for I find it a golden road to
Samarkand, when in doubt, to fling admiration at
a hoped-for friend's head. Thus dinner wore to
an end.

The men stayed no time over their wine and at
9.30 by the clock Stopford Brooke took his
departure, to the intense relief of all present
except poor me, who, regardless of convention,
followed our guest downstairs. As the hall door
was opened and he was about to go out, I seized
his hand. " Oh, Mr. Brooke," I said, " do let
me go and see your sister and your daughters."
He bowed and smiled. " But yes ! " he said,
heartily. " Delighted." " When—oh, when ? "
I inquired ; " to-morrow ? " " Certainly ! " he
went on ; " come to tea—half-past four." " Oh,

I will! half-past four," I echoed, releasing his hand and banging the front door to, so that he could not change his mind.

Such conduct on my part was inexcusable. But my existence among uncivilized races had taught me one thing—if you want anything very much, get it the best way you can.

The next afternoon I set off in the carriage for Stopford Brooke's house, No. 1, Manchester Square—such an easy address to remember! When I arrived, there he was, looking out for me. He came out to the front door and led me upstairs into the drawing-room, where his sister Cecilia was, with three of his daughters, who were quite young—Honor, Maud and Verona. Lovely pictures hung on the walls, by Millais, Ruskin, Whistler and others, whilst any number of books were to be seen about the room. Such a nice party, so what you might call " un-smart " (I hate the word " smart ") and un-Londony! Stopford Brooke made all conversation so easy and interesting—wonderful as he was, he never let one feel inferior to him in his knowledge of any subject. His handsome face was so mobile in expression and, dear me ! he was so full of energy, so *alive*, and had such an exquisite sense of humour. " Look here," he said to me that afternoon, as he handed me my tea, " we must be related, you know. You spell Brooke with an ' e ' and so do we." " How nice ! " I said. " Let us fumble a bit at our ancestral vegetable, called

by some, I believe, a family tree, and find out ! "
Cecilia and the others giggled at my words and
then he said, " Stop laughing, and don't be silly.
We both spell Brooke with an ' e '—we say we are
cousins—what more is wanted ? "   " Oh, lovely ! "
I said, " and I shall always call you my best
cousin ! "   We were all getting on well.   Then
Honor piped out, " Oh yes, and we will call each
other by our Christian names.   What is your
name ? " she asked, turning to me.   " Well," I
said, " until I married, my real name was Ghita,
culled by my French friends out of Marguerite,
but the Rajah thought Ghita too sentimental and
insisted on calling me Margaret, as being a more
correct and serious name.   But," I hastened to
add, " I hate the name of Margaret—it is ugly
and my Malay friends never liked it."   " You
will always be Ghita to us," they said—so nice of
them, I thought, and I thanked them.   Then a
very Babel of Christian names sounded through
the room.   We ladies all embraced each other
and swore eternal friendship, a friendship which
really came to pass.   How I did enjoy myself
that day !   When I left, Stopford Brooke took me
to the carriage.   " Good-bye, my best cousin,"
he said, " and do come again soon."   I took his
hand, squeezed it, and, determined to go one
better, replied, " Au revoir, mon cher ami."   As
it was in French, it did not really matter, nor
did he seem to mind—for he knew what I
meant.

That afternoon was the prelude to many visits, although I was careful never to wear out my welcome by going too often to see them. After all, tact is needed in all real friendships in life, and naturally all intelligent people practise it. However, tact or no, our visits to each other's houses were frequent and delightful. Of course, the great man was too busy with his many avocations to spend much of his time with us, but his sister and daughters were wonderful companions. We flitted about London together, went to Museums, concerts, picture galleries and so forth, for they took the keenest interest in all that was going on. Sometimes my best cousin took me with him to his lectures to workmen and artisans, for he gave them excellent advice regarding personal matters, teaching the so-called lower classes the better and nobler lessons of life. He would also initiate them into some of the beauties of Shakespeare and the more important literature of our country. He was received everywhere with the greatest affection and enthusiasm, so kind and sympathetic was he to all, helping them to understand the need for legislation and to form their own opinions in this land where no man is a slave.

One evening after he had been especially wonderful in his address to the men, as we were leaving the hall I hooked my arm into his and, as we trudged home over the slippery pavement—it was a frosty night—I tried to tell him how deeply his words had inspired and touched me.

" I am glad, my best cousin," he said. " Only I am never satisfied with what I manage to say." " Yes," I thought, " what an absence of conceit! He is indeed a great artist!" I loved him so much I am loath to leave him now, but before doing so I must relate one funny little episode. When alone with his daughters he ought really to have been given a pinafore to wear, so utterly childlike did he become. One afternoon when I called at Manchester Square, the maid, on admitting me, left me to wander where I liked, so much at home was I made to feel. Hearing an extraordinary noise of thumpings and bangings issuing from the dining-room, I opened the door and looked in. There was Stopford on top of the oak dresser, preparing to jump down, alpenstock in hand. Cecilia and the others, similarly equipped, were bounding about from chair to chair or taking leaps in order to reach the top of the window and hang there by one hand, the other grasping the alpenstock.

" Hallo, my best cousin; didn't hear you come in," said Stopford, after he had jumped down off the dresser. " You see," he went on, for on my arrival there was a temporary lull, " it is so foggy and dull outside that we thought we would give ourselves the impression of a walk across the Mer de Glace in Switzerland. But enough exercise for this afternoon. Come upstairs, best cousin, and have some tea." And then we all began to talk of other things as if the turning of his dining-room into a Mer de Glace were quite a proper and natural use to put it to !

It was at a dinner-party at Stopford Brooke's that I met his friend, the very greatest painter of his day, the celebrated Burne-Jones. That was a wonderful evening for me. Seated at the side of my host, I looked over at one of the loveliest visions of female beauty I had ever seen, Margaret Burne-Jones. A very young girl she was then, not yet out of her teens, fair, small-featured, delicate and lovely. And her eyes !—no one, I think, can ever have seen their like, before or since. She was also so sweet and so kind. She smiled lovelily, she talked simply and beautifully. She might have been likened to an angel from one of her father's pictures, just lent for one evening to mortals worthy of such a loan !

After dinner in the drawing-room Burne-Jones talked to me and was quite delightful. He took a friendly interest in Sarawak, and later, drawing Cecilia Brooke into the conversation, made her promise to bring me to his studio to see his pictures the next day but one. Then, like a fairy tale, it all came about. I went to Manchester Square to fetch Cecilia in my brougham and we drove along, ever so far, till we came to North End Road, up which we went to the very end, where a gate opened on to a green path leading up to the front door of his house, " The Grange." The maid admitted us into the hall, from which a flight of stairs led up to his studio, at which she knocked, and the great man came down himself towards us, palette in hand. "Glad to see you," he said. "Now," addressing Cecilia and handing her a key, "take the Ranee to the garden studio and let her see my pictures." He then went back upstairs and shut the door. "Oh, shan't we see him again?" I said to Cecilia, feeling a little disappointed. "Oh yes," said Cecilia, rather sharply, "but you can't expect a great man to come along and show off his own pictures." "Oh, can't you?" said I forlornly, conscious of having committed a breach of etiquette, and feeling that life was sometimes very difficult when it came to knowing what to do or say under different circumstances. We then walked through the large, somewhat bare drawing-room from which two doors opened into the garden, which was barred at one side by a very high wall. A lawn divided the house from the studio at the other end, and a path along the side led up to it. Near the house a large and lovely tree attracted my admiration. Was it possible?—a mulberry tree, so near streets and all the life of London! Now, I love trees, and mulberry trees almost more than any other. "Oh," said I to Cecilia. "Wait! I simply *must* walk round it." "My dear," said Cecilia again with some impatience, "we have not come to look at trees, but pictures." "Oh, I'm so sorry," said I, feeling that I had again been guilty of some blunder.

Now the time has come and I had better go

straight ahead and make a confession. The artistic side of me regarding pictures had never been educated, and I knew as little about art in painting and sculpture as any uncultured woman or child you might meet in the street, and although Burne-Jones and his daughter had made a wonderful impression on my mind on account of their personality, at that particular time art had nothing to do with my admiration. Cecilia flourished the key of the studio with a good deal of ostentation. She unlocked the door; we both went in. " Now, look about," she said, " and enjoy yourself." I did look about, and suddenly a new joy came into my life !

I was delighted beyond measure, so much so that I nearly sat down on the floor ! The pictures were so grand, so wonderfully grouped; their colouring, too, soft and exquisite, like words in the divinest poetry. But how can I describe what I felt, I who knew nothing about painting ? I should have loved to stay there for hours had the light not soon begun to wane and Cecilia been in a hurry to depart. What an enchanted place I had come to—the pictures, the garden, the mulberry tree, and inside the delightful house, the magician I had seen with his palette, rubbing beautiful things out of nothing ! As we went through the house on our way to the waiting brougham, Cecilia went upstairs to give back the key, upon which Burne-Jones himself came down, palette still in hand, to say good-bye. " Oh, thank you, thank you," said I, too shy to enlarge on what I had seen. "You must come again," he said. "Georgie would be so pleased." From that time forth our friendship grew apace. Dear Mrs. Burne-Jones ("Georgie") was kindness itself and made me welcome at "The Grange," and many an afternoon and evening did I spend with that wonderful genius, with his Georgie, his son Phil and his lovely daughter Margaret. Life was beautiful indeed. Although so ignorant of the technique of painting, I can only say that when I looked at any of Burne-Jones' pictures I felt myself wafted off to realms of delight and wonder, where the spirit of music, poetry and the magic of sunsets and starry nights made a land of delight for me to wander in. He was funny, too—such a sense of humour!—his caricatures were unique.

I met the most interesting beings at his house. The poet, William Morris, was often there and I, having revelled in his "Earthly Paradise," longed to know him. But, I don't know why, William Morris rather frightened me. "Why don't you talk to him?" Burne-Jones often used to say to me, as we sat together of an evening; and I did try to talk, but our conversations never came to much. He was tall and rather large and I felt that he was far removed from my simple remarks, in reply to which he used to look down at me, scratch his head and say "Oh!" I think I rather bored him, but I used to console myself with the thought that it was not given to many to be a success with such a great man as William Morris. However, I came upon more responsive beings too! William Rothenstein, who was then very young and later developed into Sir, a great artist also. Of course we made friends. *He* did not scratch his head at my remarks and say " Oh! " Grateful am I indeed that our friendship has lasted to this day. Lady Paget, also, wandered in and out, that grande dame of important embassies, whose daughter, Lady Windsor, was then being immortalized on canvas by Burne-Jones. Then the Kiplings came along —that charming gentleman, Rudyard Kipling's father; the immortal Rudyard also, who, although at that time only about twenty, had already made himself famous with *Under the Deodars*. *He* did not say " Oh! " to me either, but very freely expressed his disapproval on hearing that I had made friends in Paris with Guy de Maupassant and admired his books! Being then advanced in my thirties I said, " My dear little boy, mind your own business! " Only think of it!—I blush at my repartee now! Thus I went on with my life in England, bolstered up by the kindest and most sympathetic friends.

One afternoon, on calling at " The Grange," I found that a certain degree of excitement was disturbing the usually placid household. A

season of French plays was being given in London
and the " Divine Sarah " herself had written to
Burne-Jones suggesting that she should pay a
visit to him at his house. Now Georgie could
not speak French, and in any case had to be away
from home on the day of the proffered visit.
Burne-Jones did not quite know what to do about
it, and Georgie asked my advice. Realizing her
difficulties, and as I had often met Sarah in Paris
at the Princess of Monaco's house, I suggested
that I should fetch the lady from her hotel and
bring her to " The Grange " to tea. Georgie,
rather relieved, agreed to this plan. Arrangements were accordingly made, and on the afternoon appointed, I hired a coupé, having just then
no conveyance of my own, and went to call for
Sarah at her hotel. I found her standing on the
steps waiting for me, surrounded by a group of
male admirers. She wore a rose-coloured hat,
piled high with pink ostrich feathers, a rose-
coloured feather boa round her neck and a gown
of rose-coloured tissue, rustling with frills and
furbelows. The sight of her hat caused me some
anxiety as I feared the plumes would prove too
high for my modest coupé. This was indeed the
case and poor Sarah had to sit with her head
bent the while our drive lasted. As we were
drawing out of the courtyard of the hotel I noticed
an enormous open barouche, with coachman and
footman, *en tricorne*, on the box, and imagined

that the Lord Mayor was probably being received at some special function inside the building.

We could not talk much during the drive, Sarah's feathers causing her too much anxiety. Arrived at " The Grange," it was all plain sailing. Phil Burne-Jones had come to support his father, and I interpreted compliments and mutual admiration noises as best I could. We sat down to tea. " Délicieux ! " said Sarah, little finger lifted in the air. " Comme je suis bien ici ! " inserting tiny bits of sugared cake between her lips.

A bowl of forget-me-nots stood on the tea-table. Sarah abstracted from it a small bunch of the flowers, pushed half of them down her corsage, put the others to her lips, and then, leaning forward, poked them down Burne-Jones' waistcoat. This evidently disconcerted him. As though inadvertently, I dropped my teaspoon on the floor. As he stooped to pick it up, our heads met. " Kiss her," said I. " No," said he. " Her hand," I breathed. The hand was kissed and the situation saved ! This proved to be the *clou* of the occasion. Sarah rose to go. " Shall I take you back in the coupé ? " I asked. " But no ! I do not want to give you the trouble," said Sarah as she bade me good-bye. " I told my carriage to call for me." Burne-Jones and Phil escorted her to the gate. There they saw a magnificent equipage awaiting her—the barouche, no doubt, that I had observed in the courtyard of

the hotel, imagining it to be the Lord Mayor's.
Alas! my poor little coupé, and Sarah's far-
reaching befeathered hat! No doubt she drove
away from "The Grange" in greater comfort
than she had arrived.

CHAPTER XX

AND now, dear me, how time slips away ! We
had been at Cornwall Gardens for several years
when the Rajah saw fit to relieve my anxiety
about money—to some extent. Revenues in
Sarawak were increasing every year and the
Treasury was able to grant me a larger allowance.
I could therefore afford to take a charming little
house in Hans Place and to indulge in some
greater comforts than heretofore. My eldest son
was about eighteen and had already been out
to Sarawak before going up to Cambridge ; my
second son, Bertram, was about sixteen and his
health was still causing me anxiety. My youngest
son, Harry, having just reached his thirteenth
year, was sent to Haileybury—at which school
the Honourable Edward Lyttelton was then
Headmaster. How miserable I felt that day I
took Harry to school, when, after having tea with
the Headmaster, I bade him good-bye and saw
his beloved straw hat disappear behind the palings
of the School playground ! I wondered was he
very unhappy too ? but no ! I took courage when
I saw him engaged in conversation with another
straw-hatted youth—they were evidently making
friends. His companion had a charming face

and the friendship begun then between Harry and Guy Hodgkinson (that was his name) lasted until Harry went his way a few years ago from this life. Guy Hodgkinson distinguished himself during the Great War, and I always look upon him as one of my most beloved friends.

How funny life is, and how strangely friends seem to pop out at one here and there from the most unexpected places! Now, I have always thought that if my husband had made friends and sought the company of those in power in England, as he so easily might have done, one of the dearest wishes of his heart—that of the recognition at the English Court of the true status of Sarawak's ruler—would have come to pass much earlier than was the case. But no! In such matters he was adamant. He stood alone, wanted no friends except in Sarawak, where he was adored by his staff of English officers and his subjects, Dyak and Malay. He repelled any attempts at friendship made by people who were well disposed to him and refused invitations from those who could have been of great service to him. Although, when in England, he was in the habit of paying visits to the Prime Minister and the Chiefs at the Foreign Office and so on, I often wondered what happened at those interviews and whether the great Englishmen realized or appreciated much of what he was talking about. They were certainly aware that he was the head of the Protectorate of Sarawak, that the country was well governed,

quiet, prosperous and peaceful, but what he considered himself to be in England must have been
a riddle to all concerned—if indeed the question
ever entered their heads—for he never took the
trouble to explain.   Poor dear, he was not in any
sense a man of the world and I imagine that he
shrank from the idea of appearing to suggest his
own aggrandisement.

When, during the London season, my husband
very rightly wished to pay his respects to Her
Majesty and attend a Levée, instead of following
the example of all potentates and sending an
A.D.C. to the Lord Chamberlain's Office to
make all the necessary arrangements, he, ignorant
of worldly affairs, or the usual procedure, wrote
simply saying that he was Rajah of Sarawak and
desired to attend the Levée and signed his letter
C. Brooke.   Now, what were they to do ?   It was
not surprising that they sent a card of command
addressed to Mr. C. Brooke, appending " Rajah
of Sarawak " rather in the manner of an afterthought.   He was very angry.   " But, Charlie,
what else can they do, when you approach
them as ' C. Brooke ' ?   What do they know or
care about ' C. Brooke ' ?   Why don't you set
about things properly and in a dignified way as
befits your country and its importance ?   You
haven't *told* anyone about Sarawak and its government nor reminded them of its position."   " They
ought to know all about it *without* my telling them.
And in any case you had better mind your own

business." So there it all was. The whole question interested me much, although for my own part my precedence at dinner-parties given by some of my dear friends worried me not at all, and it was nothing to me if Mrs. FitzDoodle or the wife of a former mayor was handed her soup plate before me. But I fully sympathized with my husband and agreed with him that his position at Levées was important as Ruler of Sarawak and that his country should receive proper recognition at Court.

Now, while I quite approve of women having the vote—for they are not imbeciles!—I particularly dislike females who turn themselves into bad imitations of men, sit in Parliament, or shriek at crowds about affairs better handled by men, for, in my opinion, by so doing they lose half their power, which, after all, consists in persuasion, kind words and often very good advice. Although no one was more aware than myself of my own ignorance and shortcomings in many matters, I found myself, as I went about the world, surrounded by dear friends who were kind enough to say that they took an interest in Sarawak through knowing me. And I began to imagine that I might be of assistance to my husband in the attainment of his wish. To my great joy, my husband's first cousin, Lady Londonderry, invited us both to stay for ten days at her charming home at Machynlleth, where, as a young girl, I had spent many happy days. I had to go alone, as my husband was steadfast in his refusal to be of the party. There I met Countess Feodora and Countess Valda Gleichen, who afterwards became the dearest friends of my life. Countess Feo, as all the world knows, was a wonderful sculptor and Countess Valda possessed a beautiful voice. She sang and I played her accompaniments. What a lovely time it was! Oddly enough, both Lady Feo and Lady Valda had heard something of Sarawak from their father, Prince Victor of Hohenlohe-Langenburg, who had, during his Naval career, been officer in H.M.S. " Dido," sent under command of Captain Sir Harry Keppel to Sarawak to rid its coast of pirates. When I returned to London from this delightful visit, I found my poor husband more bored than ever with his surroundings, and he soon afterwards left England to go back to Sarawak.

I must say I enjoyed my life in London very much. Somehow I came to know many musicians. Karl Derenburg, amongst others, a wonderful amateur violinist ; Mr. Somers Cocks, an amateur 'cellist, whom we christened Piatti in joke. I played the piano and we fiddled away at classical trios to our hearts' content. Countess Valda sang for us. It was all very *gemütlich*, as the Germans have it. Then I came to know the Blumenthals, who had lovely musical parties, and Lady Lytton's sister, Mrs. Earle, who, as the French say, "*faisait la pluie ou le beau temps*" in a certain set. She never allowed tiresome or worldly folk within her doors. Alec Yorke was a cousin of hers and became my great friend. Then one evening, oh joy! I found there Henry James, who wished to be introduced to me. At the period of our first meeting he had already written *Roderick Hudson*, *Daisy Miller* and *Princess Casamassima*. When, though trembling in every limb at my own courage, I ventured to tell him what delight these books had given me, "No," he said, "my dear lady, no," lifting up his right hand outstretched in the air, "I can do better—I can do better than that." "Oh, how can you say so?" said I, "surely they are *quite* perfect?" The hand came down. He looked at me with a pitying smile. "Well, as you will! But why are you here? You come from a land where the bul-bul sings." "How did you know that?" I said. Then I told him about my three sons, that I was supervising their education, that one of my boys was causing me anxiety on account of his health and that, for the present, he had to remain in bed. He looked very sympathetically at me, asked me where I lived and whether he might come and see me. "Oh, do," I gasped out delightedly. "When?" He did not answer, said good-night, shook my hand and left me. The very next afternoon, as I was having tea in the drawing-room, "Mr. Henry James" was announced. After he had greeted me he asked if my man-servant might bring in a few parcels which he had left in his hansom. He then informed me that he had brought some puzzles, a few mechanical toys and two or three books which he thought might interest a young boy lying in bed. "Some day, let me know if he would like to see me." I felt so touched that I could hardly thank him. Needless to say, Bertram was eager to be introduced to him. He came to see him frequently, and those happy visits helped the boy to forget his troubles and did him a great deal of good. Apparently the greater the artist in painting, literature or what not, the greater within them is the thing we call a heart. I shall never forget Henry James' kindness to me and mine.

Notwithstanding the optimistic view which our family doctor at first took of Bertram's health, it became apparent to myself and my friends that another opinion was necessary, and his doctor acquiescing, he himself sought further advice. When the two medicos had consulted together, they came to the conclusion that the underlying cause of my son's continued illness came from a gouty tendency, and prescribed the very simplest and most restricted diet for him along with the maximum of fresh air. Now, although our house in Hans Place was pleasantly situated and comfortable enough, it was not altogether suitable for an invalid, and the Rajah telegraphed permission to me from Singapore to rent a house further out of London, where the air was purer, and yet not

too far off from the two doctors who were treating
Bertram. Wimbledon was suggested, and thither
I proceeded in search of a suitable abode. Mr.
Frank Schuster, a great friend of mine, was of the
greatest help in this matter. Together we inter-
viewed agents, hunted about and climbed up and
down endless flights of stairs in various houses,
until at last we found what Mr. Schuster declared
to be the very thing. Not a pretty house, but a
large, recently built suburban-looking villa, it stood
on the top of a hill, had plenty of rooms and was
surrounded by a pretty garden. Mr. Schuster
concluded the arrangements with the house agent
(thank goodness for that !) and all went well.

Bertram was pleased with our new home ; his
health, to my great joy, appeared to improve, and
very soon he was able to walk about the garden,
his doctors all the while attending him and treating
him for gouty symptoms. Then began in our
new neighbourhood *traits d'union* from friends
in London. Amongst others Mrs. Wingfield, a
delightful lady with two young daughters, came
to see us. She lived in a large house almost
across the road. On her first visit she was accompanied by her daughter Katie, and Bertram and I
both enjoyed meeting them. When they were
leaving, Mrs. Wingfield had got as far as the hall,
but Katie lingered behind, and, after taking my
hand to say good-bye, she asked whether she
might come and see me the next morning. " Oh
yes," I said—" do ! " and we left it at that.

Next morning Katie Wingfield duly appeared, and when she asked me if we could be alone, as the matter she wanted to discuss was private, I took her into the library, which was especially reserved for my own use. We seated ourselves and I asked her what she wanted to tell me. She was a charming young girl, with a slim figure, delicate features, beautiful dark eyes and wavy brown hair. " Forgive me for being inquisitive, but what do the doctors say is the matter with your son ? Without a doubt he is very ill." " Has anyone told you about him ? " I inquired, rather surprised at the turn of the conversation. " No," she replied, " no one has told me anything : but I received a message yesterday, during my visit here, acquainting me with the fact." " Please tell me," said I, " how that came to pass." " Well," she said, " the matter is rather difficult to explain, especially to people who have never studied occult forces. Will you take in good part what I am going to say ? " " Why, yes," said I, eager to listen, mark and learn. " Please go on." " Well, when I went home yesterday, after receiving the strong impression regarding your son's illness, a still more urgent message came to me when I was alone in my room. I felt impelled to get a piece of paper and a pencil, whereupon my hand, automatically driven across the sheet, wrote down a message which I have brought with me to show to you." She handed me a sheet of paper covered with slight, feathery, delicate writing which I found it difficult at first to decipher. " I will read it to you," said Katie Wingfield. " These are the words. ' Tell the lady her son is being wrongly treated, his present condition has been wrongly diagnosed. He is not suffering from gout, but from the consequences of an accident which injured his spine. His mother should consult W. B. Bennett.' " Amazed, I did not know what to say. " How did you get to know all this ? " I asked. " You only saw us yesterday for the first time." " I was made aware of it all," she said, " by an old friend of mine, a doctor, who has come into my life during the last few years. He lived two thousand years ago and his name is Semiris. He is a Greek, and is better at diagnosing an illness than any living doctor I know." Although I had had many surprises in my life I do not imagine I had ever had a greater one than hearing from this young girl about her confabs with a doctor who had departed this world two thousand years ago ! " Oh, thank you so much," I said, somewhat gauchely. " I will look into it all and see what can be done." Very tactfully she did not unduly press the matter but took leave of me and went her way.

Thenceforward I began to watch Bertram with greater solicitude than ever. In spite of the change to Wimbledon he did not appear to continue his first improvement or to gain strength. I began to lose confidence in his doctors. Miser-

able and ill at ease, I consulted Mr. Harry
Higgins—again a friend in need; thank God my
life has been full of them! He took the burden
of this matter off my shoulders and soon arranged
for one of the best known specialists in London
to come to Wimbledon. Bertram underwent a
thorough examination, the result of which proved
that gout had nothing whatever to do with his
illness, but that it was due to the injury to the
spine caused by his accident. The treatment was
altered and Bertram soon improved in health.
Now I do not wish to appear superstitious or
given to belief in supernatural manifestations, but
I could not completely rid myself of the wonderment I felt regarding the warnings of Katie
Wingfield's doctor friend who had left this world
so long ago!

After a few months' careful nursing by a
charming and thoroughly competent professional
nurse, Bertram was able to be wheeled about
Wimbledon Common in a bath chair. On his
way to and fro he had frequently seen the great
poet Swinburne, who lived at Putney, emerging
from a paper shop, his pockets stuffed with news-
papers and magazines. At that time Bertram
was very fond of reading penny-a-liners, shilling
shockers and easy literature of that kind, and
whenever I would suggest his reading more serious
works he would wax somewhat cross and reply
that he surely could not follow a better example
than that of Swinburne, whose pockets were

bulging with just that lighter sort of literature. It so happened that the mother of my kind and very musical friend, Mr. F. Schuster, lived at Wimbledon and frequently gave delightful garden parties to which I was invited. One day at one of those parties, a friend pointed out to me a lady who was walking about the lawn. "That is Lady Ritchie," she said. "She wrote that book *The Village on the Cliff*." "Oh, Anne Thackeray!" I cried. "How wonderful! Just imagine my meeting the author of that exquisite story after all those years! In Sarawak I cried myself ill reading it, I loved it so. Do, do introduce me," I said, "it would be so kind." I was then led up to the lady, who, although no longer young, was gracious and altogether charming. "Please wait a bit," said I in a tactless manner, seeing a crowd of admirers surround her, longing for a few words. "Don't mind *them*—I have so much to say!" She was naturally rather startled, but I did not care. "You come from Sarawak," she said. "I once met the first Rajah—he was a very great man." "Yes, I do come from Sarawak," I said. "I lived there for years and I want to tell you about your book—*The Village on the Cliff*. I was brought up in France and love the country, and when I read your story out in Sarawak it made me cry and cry. The *mal du pays* got hold of me and I had to stay in bed for two whole days." "My dear," she said, "all this is very nice and now we *must* be friends!" How lovely it all was and the way it had come to pass that I had really met her! That very evening I took the book out to read to Bertram, and once more I began to cry so that I had to take it away and finish it by myself in my bedroom! After that, dear Lady Ritchie and I used to visit each other often.

One morning, before I started to drive into London, I went to say good-bye to Bertram and found him looking a bit off-colour. "Is there anything I can bring you back from town?" I asked. "Oh, no," he said—"you can't get me what I really want. I want to know Mr. Swinburne." "My *dear*," I said, "how can I get you Mr. Swinburne!" "No, I don't suppose you can, but he looks *such* a good sort with all those papers sticking out of his pocket!" I did not want to refuse any of my boy's wishes, but to get hold of Swinburne was rather a colossal task. As luck would have it, Lady Ritchie came to the door just as I was about to get into my carriage. Needless to say I sent it back to the stables and begged her to come in. "And how is Bertram?" she asked. "Not very bright to-day," I replied. "I know, of course, that invalids are apt to be a bit unreasonable and ask for the impossible, but really——!" "Oh, what impossible thing is he asking for?" "Nothing more or less than to know Mr. Swinburne!" "Well," said Lady Ritchie, "order your carriage at once and we will go to Putney, get Mr. Swinburne and bring him back." Now, had the brightest star in all the heavens fallen at my feet and turned itself into a diamond for me to wear, I could not have been more astonished or delighted. Bertram's wish granted and the wonderful experience of sitting in the same carriage with the creator of such passionate, tender and exquisite lines—the magician composer of " Dolores " and so many other poems which simply lift one's soul up to Paradise and turn one's heart inside out! Oh dear, how could such a thing come to pass!

However, we got into the carriage and drove down to the poet's residence, " The Pines." We both got out; Lady Ritchie marched up the steps resolutely and quite sure of herself, while I tiptoed meekly after her, so that even the stones should not imagine I took anything for granted. " Yes," said the maid, in answer to Lady Ritchie's inquiry, Mr. Swinburne was at home; and she led the way upstairs, knocked at a door on the landing and a voice said " Come in." We entered, and there we stood, Lady Ritchie and I, in the presence of the poet. Everyone in England knows what Mr. Swinburne was like, so I will not attempt to describe his appearance excepting to say that his hair was redder in colour than I had imagined it and that he was not as tall as I had thought. My eyes were glued to his face. Every feature seemed to me to radiate genius, while his eyes, although piercing and alert, seemed to be full of all the glory and beauty of the world.

"Dear Lady Ritchie," he said, "a pleasant surprise! And your friend the Ranee. Yes, the first White Rajah endowed this country with one of the most beautiful stories of the world." We were getting on very well and then, as now, I realized with gratitude how much of my success was due to the fact that I was enveloped in a tiny fold of that great man's mantle! Then Lady Ritchie said, "My friend's son is ill in bed and must be for some time an invalid. He has read some of your poems and has, from his bath chair, seen you going backwards and forwards and he does so *wish* he could know you!" "Does he really want to see me?" said Mr. Swinburne and looked at me. I murmured something unintelligible. "Well," he said, "of course I'll come, and at once. But let me first just get my boots." (He was wearing red flannel slippers.) "Where *are* my boots?" he went on impatiently. "They are somewhere in this room, I know." We then all began searching for his boots. Anxious to show zeal, I got on a chair and looked among the higher bookshelves for them. Swinburne himself sought for them behind lower shelves, knocking tomes on to the floor in so doing. When at last a shout from Lady Ritchie proclaimed victory, they were lying inside an empty coal-scuttle! On went the boots (they were elastic-sided), the red flannel slippers being kicked aside. The poet's hat was hanging in the hall. He put it on and quickly followed us into the brougham.

What a splendid afternoon! Only fancy driving Swinburne back from Putney to one's very own house!

I need not expatiate on the pride and joy with which Bertram welcomed the great man. They soon became close friends. The poet came to lunch two or three times a week and, to amuse the boy and interest him, he sometimes brought a poem with him which, maybe, he had written overnight, asking Bertram to read and criticize it, even inviting him to *blue pencil portions of the verses he might not like*! Wonders will never cease! It is all so long ago that those things happened, but the great sympathy and kindness the poet showed to my invalid son, young as he was, can never fade from my memory.

Had it not been for Bertram's illness I should much have enjoyed our stay at Wimbledon. All our friends were kind and often came to see me. Our Sunday parties were sometimes very amusing —especially when Lady de Grey brought with her a contingent of musicians such as Calvé, and Jean and Édouard de Reszke. Lord and Lady Radnor also frequently joined our party. We were, of course, all of us good friends, the great bond of music attracting us to each other. Nevertheless, often on those Sunday evenings at Wimbledon music would be laid aside, the rival attraction being Miss Katie Wingfield, who unquestionably appeared to everyone to be a most extraordinary medium, and, in whatever manner she managed her spiritualistic demonstrations, no one who met her and saw her at work could fail to be impressed. Certainly my guests all appeared to enjoy themselves when, at a given moment, the table, at which were seated twelve or fifteen people with hands outstretched and finger-tips touching, would slowly rise in the air, sometimes to a height of two or three feet, coming down again upon the very hard parquet floor as gently as though cushioned in velvet. Incoherent sentences were occasionally rapped out, so incoherent as to make me wonder sometimes that Lord Radnor, Lady de Grey and others should imagine it worth their while to listen to them with wonderment.

I did not often join in the magic circle at the table, but watched the supposed supernatural happenings from afar. One evening, however, a curious thing did happen. Certain knocks on the table were supposed to reveal the presence of Arthur Goring Thomas, who had died two years previously. A series of rhythmic knocks was heard matching the time of one of his compositions, " Winds in the Trees." Recognizing the metre, I played an accompaniment to it very softly on the piano. When I had finished, the table rapped out that Arthur Goring Thomas had left me an object in his will which I had not yet received, but which would reach me within a fortnight. I thought nothing about it at the time, but ten days later a letter reached me from

Arthur Goring Thomas' brother, whom I had never seen, informing me that he had found in a case belonging to Arthur which had not been opened since his death, a first edition of Tom Moore's poems which his brother had left me in his will. Queer!—but who knows? Someone may have been playing a trick! At any rate, although I give my opinion in all humility, I cannot believe that tables rushing about, rising in the air and rapping out incoherent sentences are the means of transmitting messages to us from those who have departed this world. If there were any truth in these " messages," surely the senders would find something more intelligent to talk to us about. But perhaps, after all, those elementary manifestations may be only the thin edge of the wedge and by and by we may, some of us, feel certain that we are able to communicate with the next world. The danger to it all being that the charlatans who attend those meetings in great numbers are apt to cheat for all they are worth in order to take in those present and get well paid for their lies.

During our pleasant stay at Wimbledon, Sir William Bennett performed a most satisfactory operation on Bertram, after which my dear son was completely restored to health. He still required care and plenty of sunshine, and the doctor advised my taking him to Italy for the winter. Then a villa had to be sought for. My great friend the Princess of Monaco asked some friends of hers living near Genoa to look out for a suitable house for me, and they succeeded in finding one high up on the top of a hill not far from Nervi, at Bogliasco. It was a nice little abode, painted white with yellow shutters and had a lovely view over the Mediterranean and its cliff-bound coasts, to which clung olive woods, even rose gardens dipping themselves into the sea. Sometimes we were pleased, sometimes rather sorry, that we were but one mile removed from Nervi, where an enormous hotel harboured portions of the beau-monde from Russia, Austria and elsewhere. A few introductions from friends were the means of our becoming acquainted with Italians here and there who possessed villas. Amongst others the Gropallos, two daughters and one son; their father, Marchese Gropallo, a veritable Italian aristocrat, had left them, when he died, the villa where they continued to live. My son and I came to know them well and they were charming to us, as were also some Austrians whose acquaintance we made. We all became very " cliquey," the only drawback to this being that one was, willingly or no, compelled to join in any festivities our foreign friends chose to set on foot, a refusal to appear on any of those festive occasions—be you ever so weary—was to them a source of offence. Some of our friends, for instance, received every evening after dinner. Now if there was a thing I detested—not being in my first youth—it was hustling out after my evening meal, when a sofa, an interesting book or my piano were for me more congenial company than the brilliant assembly to be found at the Gropallos' or at the Hotel Nervi.

Bertram and his tutor, a charming young man who came with us to Bogliasco to prepare him for Cambridge, naturally enjoyed such nocturnal outings, but, oddly enough, the *société* thought my not being present rather snubbing on my part. On one occasion the Italian lady who was holding the reception was angry at my absence and said to my son's tutor, " And your Signora, why isn't she here ? She does give herself airs. They tell me she thinks she is a queen ! Pah ! " she went on, rapping open her fan. " Una regina de cartone ! " A cardboard queen ! One for me and no mistake ! I was much amused and wished that I could have felt like one, for I weighed the scales down twelve stone ! But I bore her no malice, poor dear, and even looked upon her annoyance at my absence as something of a compliment. I was very happy at seeing Tiny, Princess Salm, who was a great friend of mine, and Baroness Wrangel, a Russian with two delightful daughters, from whom, alas ! I have been unable to obtain news since the Russian *débâcle*. The more one travels about the world making friends here and there, the more one looks upon such friendships as lovely flowering shrubs laden with sweetness and delight. You love them dearly. Then suddenly, for no apparent reason and without warning, a disastrous tempest, coming from the unknown, uproots them ; they are destroyed and seen no more, although they live for ever in your heart.

Thus Bertram and I spent two or three years in Nervi until he was finally completely restored to health.

And where was the Rajah all this time ? some might inquire. Well, at the risk of shocking those who, prosaically inclined, imagine that matrimony should be a state of life in which husband and wife are eternally joined to one another (thus disregarding the dictation of circumstances), I must admit that my husband was just a little, and quite nicely, bored with me ! Independence was what he cared for, and a wife, if only at times, showed symptoms of wishing for domesticity, and this he really could not stand.

At that time, Bertram and I both being healthy and well, I felt an overwhelming desire to revisit my dear Sarawak, taking Bertram with me, and wrote to the Rajah to acquaint him with the fact. I must say that his reply was not very encouraging. However, my allowance now being a more ample one, and by writing blandishments to Messrs. Coutts, the most courteous and delightful of bankers, I managed to scrape up enough for Bertram's and my passage there and back. So one morning in April we boarded a North German Lloyd liner at Genoa and had a very comfortable and delightful voyage out to Singapore. There we stayed for a day or two at Government House before embarking in the Sarawak mail steamer for Kuching. The Rajah received us at the Astana landing-place, and on the whole his welcome was not enthusiastic. Never mind, I thought, it will be all right by and by. And so it was! My darling Malay women swarmed up to the house in the afternoon. They patted me affectionately. They cried and I cried, they laughed and so did I. "Come back to us, Rajah Ranee," they said. "Come and live beside us again!" We went into the garden. The peacocks were no more . . .! Of course not, after all those years. We then picked up the threads of remembrance, talking of the happy days of youth. Santubong looked majestic from the garden, showing the great Rajah's profile across the sky; Venus trembled in beauty before our eyes again. The stars came out—my beloved friends got into their boats, their paddles in the water making the rhythmic noises as of yore. We felt sad at saying good night. The friendship was there still, but the uncertainties of life, the passing away of years had worn so much of its happiness away. . . .

I am not sure that most of the Rajah's officials liked me much or cared about my coming to Sarawak, but there were three exceptions. One was Frank Maxwell and the others were Harry Deshon and Reginald Awdry. These three were most loyal friends of mine, whom of course I had known for years. One can hardly be surprised at the others or blame them, seeing the Rajah's attitude to me. Chased away from the country owing to my health and having to reside in England for years to superintend the education of my sons, my absence from Sarawak was due to no fault of mine. On the other hand, it might be difficult to understand the motives underlying the Rajah's wish to keep me away. However, let any Englishman try for a moment to put himself in his position—a position unequalled in independence by any of his countrymen. In Sarawak he was, in every sense of the word, monarch of all he surveyed. His wife bored him, necessitating certain rules, certain modes of life which he could not tolerate. He wished to remain alone and supreme in the love and affection of his subjects, which he certainly possessed whatever may have been the attitude of my Malay friends to me. His was undoubtedly a jealous nature and no one could alter that trait in his character. It was unfortunate for him and prevented him having the happier, fuller life which he would have had if he had made friends with me and with his sons, who were so full of affection. But with it all my husband and I never quarrelled. He must always have known the intense admiration I felt for his work in Sarawak, and in all matters I always remained his ally, especially in his policy of government, right down to the day

of his death. If anyone had spoken disrespect-
fully of him in my presence, such an one would
never have dared to do so again. Yes, he was a
great man, but I was sorry for him; he missed
so much. It was not through any fault of his.
He was just made so.

I need not now explain how disconcerting it
was both for Bertram and myself that just after
our arrival my husband betook himself off to
England, to Cirencester, where he had a place
from which to hunt in the winter. I hastily add
that I think he was quite right to get hunting at
home occasionally, as it helped to keep him in the
splendid health he enjoyed until the age of
eighty-five, when he departed this life, never for
one day divesting himself of his duties to Sarawak.
To his splendid reign the country owes the mak-
ings of its present prosperity. Although the
Rajah's absence from Sarawak at the time of my
visit was a great disappointment to Bertram and
myself, we managed to enjoy ourselves during
our stay. We paid several visits together to many
of my old haunts—to Simanggang, where I met
many friends: to Sibu and Kapit, where we
stayed some days and, in company with Mr.
Bampfylde, we pushed up as far as the rapids of
the Rejang, where I experienced the joy of
shooting the Belaga rapids in a small canoe,
steered by the star steerer of that neighbourhood,
an old friend of mine, a Kayan named Sali.

If anyone happens to be suffering from depression and has a bit of money to spare, let the depressed one embark on a ship to Singapore, there tranship into the mail for Kuching, find his way to Kapit, then just float on something to Belaga; climb for half a day up over the rocks of a waterfall, and at the top get into a canoe with a native steerer, leave himself in his hands—and *off* he goes! The water flashes white and dashes over rocks, great forest trees forming screens on either bank. The air is sometimes filled with pale blue butterflies and strange birds flutter overhead, whilst you glide down as in a dream, frightened now and then at huge rocks apparently about to dash you to pieces, although you go past them unharmed. The danger which seems ever present is lovely, and all too soon you reach the smooth water and are quite sorry to feel safe once more. There is nothing like it in the world!

After such delightful experiences as those of shooting the Belaga rapids alone with Sali in a canoe, feeling all the ecstasy of a swallow on the wing (although by no stretch of the imagination could any swallow have imparted its ecstasies to me, I yet feel the simile to be a correct one!), we made our way to Sibu and thence back to Kuching. There we found our great friends Mr. and Mrs. Maxwell, the Harry Deshons, Reginald Awdry and his wife, all of them lovers of Sarawak. We persuaded them to breakfast, tea and dine with us at the Astana as often as they could, for, alas! the time allowed to us by our return tickets was rapidly shrinking and only a few days remained. My dear Malay women friends visited me daily, and we talked over our many years of friendship and recalled with pleasuresome thrills the happy times we had spent together.

The virgins of other days had turned into worthy married women and become the proud mothers of hardy sons and charming maidens. Jokes of years long past were dished up again— the peacocks and the sentry's toes and many another silly delight recalled. We laughed together but we cried also, for is there anything so sad and gloomy in life as parting for ever from those we love? " Don't go away, Rajah Ranee," they kept on saying. " Stay with us here." But, alas! I realized that when I should depart this time from Sarawak, I might never see them again, for in the days I am speaking of it appeared to be an impossible thing in the Rajah's mind for me to spend a few months at a time in Sarawak, instead of remaining there for years with only an occasional holiday in England. He certainly would not have consented to such an arrangement, nor was he, as has already been shown, anxious for my presence in the country. It was indeed a very great grief to me, for I loved the land, its people, its beauty; the poetry and romance of it all were deeply embedded in my heart. And I now wonder whether, with the exception of my Malay friends, their children and grandchildren, anyone nowadays in Sarawak even remembers my name! As I close this chapter of my life out there I feel I cannot linger on such personal recollections. They make me too unhappy. I tried to give the people and the country all I could give of sympathy and love, but I may often have been tactless and rushed in ruthlessly where others feared to tread. I do not wish to be bitter, for bitterness spoils the meaning of life, and perhaps I am a bit too anxious for pattings on the back, such pattings, when a few of them are given, seldom seeming to come from the proper quarter! However, one must be philosophical and try to make the best of everything. Now that I have come to some sort of conclusion I shall leave it at that. Sentiment nowadays is looked upon by many as something of a crime, and perhaps they are right. Yet when we die and are laid away in the grave, surely by then our lonely state can do no harm to anyone alive or upset their idiosyncrasies. Very well then, maybe some day a recording angel, with pen steeped in love and beauty, may pass by where I rest and inscribe " Sarawak " in great golden letters right across my heart.

CHAPTER XXII

AFTER I had been back in England for some years, as I realized that the " sere and yellow " season of my life was not very far ahead, I felt the necessity of making myself a permanent home where my sons, now grown to men with outlooks of their own, could come and go as they pleased. Vyner was already making a name for himself in Sarawak, but would need a twig to perch on during his visits to England. Bertram had obtained a commission in the Artillery and was at that time serving in Ireland. Then my dear Harry, youngest of the three, to my great joy, elected to live with me for a time, not yet having made any serious plans for his future. With the Rajah's consent, I rented a house at Ascot, " Grey Friars," and there established myself. The Rajah eventually bought it and left it in his will to my eldest son. Quite a nice house, it was large enough to hold us all and had one or two spare rooms for friends. I found Ascot a delightful place to live in. Within a mile or so lived Lady Ponsonby, that wonderful gracious lady whom to know was to love and whose long residence at Court with Queen Victoria and intimate relations with all the Big Wigs of the day never lessened the interest she took in more humble members of English society whom, like fortunate me, she came to know and enrich with her friendship. Then there was Maggie Ponsonby, her daughter. She and I became great friends. I must leave it at that, as hundreds of my pages would not suffice to give any idea of the unvarying sympathy and help she has been to me on many occasions of difficulty. Her three brothers, John, Frederick and Arthur Ponsonby, also became my good friends and took the greatest possible interest in Sarawak. Sir Walter and Lady Palmer were neighbours of ours too, and, somewhat further off, Lord and Lady Esher. To my great delight my neighbours' houses harboured many charming damsels, lovely young girls who philandered and flirted—and quite right too!—with my sons. So good for them. Flights of fancy are needed for young men, who require a bit more amusement than that of perpetually hanging over an ageing mother's armchair. It so happened that a great friend of Harry's lived near us, Ralph Alderson. They had met at Trinity College, Cambridge, and both having strong dramatic instincts, they managed to organize private theatrical performances here and there for the benefit of various charities. It is not necessary for me to remind anyone interested in the drama of the very high standard reached by " The Windsor Strollers " or of how largely the acting of Ralph Alderson contributed to the success of these performances. I can hardly imagine that there has ever been a finer exponent of " Falstaff " in the " Merry Wives " than he. Ralph and Harry got a few friends together who were valuable additions to their company—Lady Susan Yorke, as she was in those days, Miss Olga Montagu and her sister Mary, Lady Agneta Montagu's daughters, and one or two others. They started to rehearse " The Private Secretary," performances of which were to be given at Windsor and elsewhere in aid of charities. They were progressing most satisfactorily and having great fun over it when I began to feel that I did not like to be left out. The thought came to me —an orchestra—the very thing! An orchestra is wanted in a theatre to help people to talk between the acts! Not knowing much about the musical accomplishments in the neighbourhood, I flew to Maggie Ponsonby for advice and found her standing at her hall-door. " An orchestra for the theatricals," she cried, " of course you must have one! You'll undertake the piano part. And now I'll look about and find out who can do what in a band. Come along! " She jumped at a hat hanging on a peg in the hall and bumped it on her head, where it wobbled unsafely over the thickness of her hair. She then dragged me off to the stables, ordered out her pony carriage, made me get in and galloped up the road to my door, where she told me to get out. " Where are you going ? " I asked. " I don't know, but

I'll get you things!" I felt somewhat dubious but left it at that.

A line from her next morning gave me to understand that she had collected five violins, one 'cello, a harmonium, a big drum, a side drum —and if necessary a flute, carried in side drum's pocket, who, however, had not yet *quite* mastered its notes!—a concertina and a triangle. "At any rate," she said, "you'll be able to make a noise!" and I hoped for the best! Two days later, Maggie herself marshalled her musicians into my room for a rehearsal. Meanwhile I had lost no time in procuring a dozen or more copies of Strauss's "Wein, Weib und Gesang" for the piano, and, pencil in hand, did my best to arrange each for the requirements of the different instruments. Here and there I wrote "silence all here"; "four bars of side drum"; I marked the different bits for harmonium and concertina "wind," made playful little scratches where the triangle came in and pounded down heavy circles where the big drum was to be heard. I presented each musician with a copy of the waltz, thus marked, and was surprised at the jauntiness of the result when, seated at the piano, I led them into the fray. I must say the members of my band were adorable; all pretty girls who tried so hard to do their best; and, after all, we managed to produce something out of the simple tunes chosen to meet exigencies. Gladys Palmer, playing the triangle, and Sylvia Brett the big drum, tinkled and banged their ways respectively into my two sons' hearts. All went merry as a marriage bell, and soon indeed the wedding bells sounded, a bit too loudly in my ears, for my two sons naturally deserted me for their wives, which was only to be expected and quite as it ought to be. Then, some years later, my dear Harry fell in love with Dorothy Craig, a niece of Lady Palmer. They were married and I was left quite alone. Poor Dorothy! She was a darling and lovely exceedingly, but always delicate. She lived but a few years in married happiness and died of consumption, leaving Harry sorrowful indeed. Meanwhile the Rajah very much appreciated and approved of his daughters-in-law. We appeared together at the weddings and the ladies grew to like him well. He lived by that time at Cirencester, where, on his well-earned holidays from Sarawak, he enjoyed his favourite sport of hunting.

About that time the Rajah received a communication from the Lord Chamberlain wherein it was made known to him that King Edward had decreed that his status as Ruler of an Independent State under British protection should be recognized in England and that in future he would be received at Court as His Highness the Rajah of Sarawak and be given precedence just after the Ruling Princes of India. My kind friend, Sir Frederick Ponsonby, who knew of my husband's wonderful work for his country, had spoken to King Edward on the subject and thus the question was settled by his late Majesty once and for all.

My life at Ascot without my sons was very lonely. I read a great deal and Henry James was very kind in placing his library at my disposal. I often used to visit his flat in London, on the Embankment, and was free to go in and out of his library whether he was at home or no. One afternoon when I went there his servant, on letting me in, showed me into the dining-room and told me that his master would join me presently. I went and sat down by the window from where I could see the barges on their way up and down the river. By and by the great man came in. Such a wonderful apparition! Over his ordinary clothes he wore a sumptuous Japanese kimono embroidered with large golden storks. "My dear, my dear," he said, with uplifted hand, "that I should dare receive you thus! In this room, too, and all because the drawing-room has a better light!" "Dear Master," I said, "I don't mind. But what have you been about?" "Been about? dear Lady" (hand still waving in the air). "I have been in the company of an ignoble, horrible being, the name of whose calling shall not assail your ears! So low, so despicable!" he went on, rolling off many other adjectives which I have forgotten by now. "But who *was* it, Master?" said I. "If I say it, dear Lady, forget it! Forget it as soon as spoken! Well—

it was . . ." (then a pause) " the chiropodist."
" But never mind, dear Master, the question of
toes makes the whole world kin ! " " Toes ! "
he said. " Pah ! ! ! But wait," he went on, " we
will have some tea and then go into the library."
After tea, when we were among his books, I
saw, on one of the higher shelves, an exquisitely
bound volume with E L I A standing out in
great gold letters. " What a lovely binding ! "
said I as I proceeded to climb up some steps
standing on the parquet floor. " E, L, I, A,"
I spelled aloud ; " what does it mean ? " (I
knew about Charles Lamb's Essays, but, not
being literary, had not heard t'other name.)
Henry James bounced up from his chair. " What
does it mean ? What a darling you are—like
nobody ! "—and, scrambling up the other side
of the double ladder, he was about to clasp me
round the neck when the steps, not being properly
fastened, slid apart over the slippery floor.
Tableau ! ! Henry James on one side, and me on
the other, both on our stomachs, our feet kicking
in the air ! We extricated ourselves with some
difficulty, I barking my shins considerably in
doing so. On reaching a standing position I
laughed and laughed—I could not help it, but the
poor dear stood there and never even smiled.
" An ignominious position ! " he deplored, and
was astonished when I said, " What on earth does
it matter ? *I* don't care ! " He never alluded
to it again.

The years slipped away and then the awful
war came. I believe that, like so many others,
the horror Henry James felt at it all helped to
undermine his health. During his last days he
became naturalized an Englishman, and an overwhelming joy it was to him when he was presented
with the Order of Merit. When he died a great
deal of happiness was taken out of my life, for we
were very great friends and indeed he is still daily
in my thoughts.

Whilst I lived at Ascot I made another very
dear friend, W. H. Hudson, and I imagine all will
agree that he was an outstanding representative
of English literature. I came to know him in a
somewhat unconventional way. Although, as I
have said, I am by no means what might be called
"literary," I am never so happy as when reading,
and at the very beginning of this century came
across, in the *Saturday Review,* a criticism of a
book called *Green Mansions* by W. H. Hudson.
This criticism, by Mrs. Cunninghame Graham,
enthralled me. What the gifted lady had to say
about it simply set me agog with excitement, and
I immediately telegraphed for it to Bickers, my
bookseller, who despatched it to me forthwith.
I at once began it, and can never describe my
feeling on reading it except to say that I thought
it one of the loveliest things I had met with in
current English literature. So tender, so beautiful,
so close to Nature ! You could almost scent the
fragrance of tropical vegetation as you went

through its pages. Here and there the cruelty
and ugliness of flesh-eating individuals ; and then
the purity, simplicity and divinity of Rima—
half bird, half woman ! I had to stay awhile over
the poignancy of its last pages. I could think of
nothing but *Green Mansions* for days. It obsessed
me. I read it over and over again and determined
that I must somehow or other meet face to face
the author of this wonderful book. I inquired of
all my literary friends, " Do you know the author
of *Green Mansions ?* " No, I found no one who
did. About that time I went, as I did most years
when summer was on the wane, to stay with some
kind friends in Essex, who lived off the beaten
track—Lady Pennefather and Miss Guinness. We
shared the same tastes and I always looked forward
with pleasure to the fortnight I spent with them
every year. On the last evening of my visit I
was rather bored to find that a lady whom I did
not know had come to dine. When we went in
to dinner she and I sat on either side of our host.
I was just about to dip my spoon into the soup
when something made me aware that the new-
comer was a friend of Hudson. My spoon still
in the air, I caught and fixed her eye. " You
know W. H. Hudson," I said, " the author of
Green Mansions." " Yes, I do," she replied in
rather a surprised tone, " but how did you know
I did ? He is such a retiring man and holds
himself aloof from everyone." " It came into
my mind that you did. And now that you *do*

know him, do please arrange that I may know him too." "That would be impossible," she replied, " he will not meet anybody." I thought it better not to wrangle over the dinner-table, so said no more; but later, when the ladies were alone in the drawing-room, I returned to the subject. "Look here," said I to the lady, with my best smile, " you really must manage somehow that I get to know Hudson." "Well, if you really *mean* it," she replied (somewhat sillily, I thought), " you would have to come to tea at my flat and pretend that you were staying with me. I could send you a wire next time I am expecting him to come and see me." She was a kind lady and I gladly fell in with her plan. Next day she went back to London and I returned to Ascot. About a week later I received the telegram and hied myself off to London. Arriving at the lady's flat about half-past three, I took off my hat and tried to look as much at home and as innocent as possible. As the clock on the mantelpiece chimed the half-hour after four, Hudson arrived. On seeing me he frowned slightly until it was explained to him that I was staying with my hostess, having come to London to consult a doctor. "You are Rajah Brooke's wife," he said. "Have you lived out in Sarawak ?" (Shades of my beloved Rajah !) "Yes," I said. And after that he and I got on like a house on fire. We actually made plans for future meetings ! He would be at the R.S.P.B.'s rooms, then in Hanover

Square, two afternoons later and would show me pictures and books about birds.

Thus began another and lovely friendship. W. H. Hudson, although at that time about seventy years of age, was still very handsome. Tall and spare, he was one of the most active men I had ever met. His face was long and thin with high cheek-bones, his nose was aquiline, his beard and moustache short, while his piercing eyes, dark and beautiful, reminded me of an eagle. Like so many other really great authors, he was very modest, and appeared to be unaware of the excellency of his writings. He came to stay with me often at Ascot, taking great pleasure in the pinewoods which stretched out in all directions beyond my garden at " Grey Friars." During one of his visits he was much excited at the appearance of a pair of large hawks, somewhat rare birds for that part of the country, which had built their nest some forty feet from the ground in a branch of a fir tree near by. One pouring wet evening, on coming home to " Grey Friars " for tea, I met Hudson at the hall door in the greatest state of excitement, pointing to a ladder fixed against the hawks' tree. " Look here," he said. " I sent to Sunningdale for this ladder. Do just run up it and see what the nest is like inside. I can't trust anyone else, they would see nothing, and I can't go myself because I've hurt my knee." He evidently thought the request quite an ordinary one and was somewhat surprised and annoyed when I declined to comply with it. Next day, when the ladder was called for and carried away unused, he was very disappointed. I was sorry, but no! at my age I dared not venture such a gymnastic feat!

Another friend who was very kind to me was Dorothy Brett. Although quite young at that time, she was an artist even then, and all know by now how much her paintings are appreciated and admired in America and elsewhere. Alas! she has left England and lives almost entirely in New Mexico. But in the days I write of, when she was within reach in England, we spent some happy weeks during the late summer in the lovely little Wiltshire riverside village called Wiley. Hudson often came over to see us, as he was staying only a mile or two away. We all three used to go for walks; but one afternoon he and I went alone, Dorothy having gone to Salisbury. We were crossing a great green meadow in which four or five hunters had been put out to grass. Beautiful they were, and one of the splendid creatures, a chestnut, came up to me, snuffing kindly at my arm and blowing that loveliest of all scents—a healthy horse's breath—into my face. Suddenly Hudson said, " I shall get on him." " Surely not! " I said, but seeing that Hudson was hoisting himself on the horse's back (by his tail, I think!) I stepped aside. The animal, resenting this unwonted familiarity, began bucking, kicking and rearing, but Hudson sat like a centaur, lightly handling his mane. Then he was borne away, round and round the field until his hat fell off, when he stopped the horse somehow, got off, picked up his hat, placed it on his head and joined me. My astonishment made me silent for a time. Then, as we were letting ourselves out of the field, Hudson carefully closing the gate, I said, " Do you often do that sort of thing, and why ? " " What a question ! " he said ; " why bother about it ! Please don't allude to the matter again." And there the subject dropped. I remembered that as a boy he had been brought up in the Pampas—not far from Buenos Aires, where once upon a time his father had a ranch and where I knew that youths were accustomed to break in wild prairie horses to the saddle. But, after all, it was a wonderful sight to see !

One day a friend of mine just back from Cornwall came to have tea with me at Ascot. She had been staying about three miles from St. Ives, at a village called Lelant, where, she told me, fields of violets bloomed right through the winter months. How heavenly, I thought ; I must one day go there ! A day or two later, Harry, coming in to see me, told me he had stayed there not long ago, having made the acquaintance of two charming ladies—the Misses Sealy—who had been kind and hospitable to him. Being then, alas ! very much my own mistress, I made up my mind to go there, and with Harry's intro- duction, wrote asking the Misses Sealy if they would be able to get me rooms in April. They were kindness itself, and when April came I went down and simply revelled in the beauty of that charming spot and my pleasure in Maud and Hilda Sealy's companionship. We excursioned together, sat on cromlechs on lovely moors, drove through lonely valleys and along deserted roads, for ever feeling that sense of mystery and charm that Cornwall yields to those who have found her heart. The Cornish people too, what darlings they are! Just walk through a Cornish village, leaving any sense of superiority (if you are given that way) behind, and you can make friends for life with every man, woman and child you chance to meet with.

That first stay of mine lasted a month, and I left the lovely land with regret, promising myself to revisit it in the winter. I did so for two or three years, renting houses here and there and coming to love Lelant more and more every time I came back to it.

And then, whilst I was living at Ascot, that dire catastrophe, War, enveloped us all as in a pall. My darling Bertram joined his regiment and was sent off to Egypt to fight the Turks. Harry at once enlisted under command of Colonel Sir John Harrington, who was his friend when he was in the thick of it all on the Marne. The Rajah was at Cirencester and Vyner was taking his place in Sarawak. Notwithstanding his great age (he was then over eighty-three), the Rajah, in spite of the dangers at that time attending sea voyages, insisted on going back to the East, and when he returned to England a year or so later his health gave way and he died at Cirencester at the age of eighty-five.

Death came easily to him, for he realized that he had left Sarawak in the safe keeping of his son, with the additional security of Bertram, who dearly loves the country and knows the people and their ways. The two brothers are devoted to one another, and Vyner, although lacking a son of his own, is happy in having a brother and two nephews staunch and loyal towards his policy, thus ensuring the well-being of Sarawak in days to come.

Some time before he died the Rajah bought me a cottage at Lelant in which to spend my winters. Surrounded by a small garden, it has a little pond with goldfish in it which is a great pleasure to me. I love to scatter crumbs to them and watch the grateful whisk of their tails. After all, I tell myself, the world is quite a nice place when one can find solace in tokens of gratitude—even from goldfish !

And now some part of what I still have to write will be dull and a little sad. I have grown into quite an old woman, and old women are not the salt of the earth. Yet one can still grieve and be nearly able to give things up as those we care for most in the world leave it for pastures new. The most terrible grief came to me only a few years

ago, when I was at Lelant. One morning a
telegram from Harry's great friend, Guy Hodgkinson, reached me with the news that Harry
had been taken suddenly ill and that an immediate
operation was to be performed. Too late to
catch the Riviera Express, I started off at once in
the car—a friend, although at that time she hardly
knew me—Miss Clara Rogers (who has since
become Lady Vyvyan of Trellowarren), insisted
on coming with me to London. We only stopped
at Exeter to give the chauffeur an hour's rest.
Arriving in London we were told that Harry was
gone. . . . What is to be said about it ! No
words can be found to bear upon such tragedies,
meted out, alas ! to so many. Harry and I were
such " pals " and he was so good to me. In a
strange way our talks were very serious ones and,
oddly enough, they were often on the subject of
death. " There is no such thing as death,
darling," he often said to me. " We just step
from one world into another. It depends on
ourselves what sort of world we step into. We
prepare for it here, every moment of our lives,
and we should try to realize that in every bit of
kindness we show and help we give to any sentient
being, there lies our safety. Knowing that, we
can enter the great Beyond without any fear."
I can write no more about this loss of mine, but
just mention the last words Harry said to his
doctor as he passed away : " Tell Mother I am
all right. . . ."

My consolation, when I ponder over many sorrows in life, comes from the wonderful kindness I have received from my friends. From Lady Vyvyan, for instance, who thought nothing of the great inconvenience to herself when she came with me from Cornwall, and returned next morning after so many hours' travel by road. Indeed, many a time and oft I have been simply bolstered up and made ready to start life afresh by the never-ending goodness of my friends.

CHAPTER XXIII

THUS I had to pick up my life again. I returned to Lelant and tried to concentrate on music, practising hard on a Beethoven Concerto I had promised to play at a concert in Penzance in aid of charity. I played the concerto, not caring much what people thought; it had given me some work to do and something to think about.

Then another charming friend, Mrs. Pennell, a neighbour of mine at Lelant, who plays the violin beautifully (having been a pupil of Joachim's), often came to my cottage, when we spun out Bach, Mozart, Beethoven and Brahms to our hearts' content. Oh yes, I am fortunate in my friends!

After I left Ascot and removed to Lelant, in Cornwall, my sons and their respective children objected to my being so far away from them all the year round, necessitating such a long journey from their homes to mine. So Vyner bought me a nice little house in Albert Road, Regent's Park, in which to live during the summer. It has a little garden and trees round it, and from the Zoo, near by, I can hear the elephants trumpeting during the night. I therefore spend the winter months in Cornwall and the rest of the time in London.

It is curious to realize how in advancing years even the smallest matters have power to rouse satisfaction or disappointment. Passing by a bird shop in London a short while ago, I saw, penned inside a cage too small for them, a pair of fantails, looking miserably cramped. I bought the birds, carried them home in the car, and had a small pigeon house erected for them on the lawn. The birds soon learned to make themselves at home. They became quite tame, flew about together, sat side by side on tree branches or on the roof of my house. I named them Romeo and Juliet, so bridal and loving did they appear. My butler, a kindly being, looks after them and sees that they are well fed. A morning or two ago, at breakfast, showing some concern, he came to me and said, " I am afraid Your Highness may experience a great disappointment ! " " Why ? " I asked. " What is the matter ? What has happened ? " " Well . . . Your Highness, I am very sorry . . . but . . . Romeo has laid an egg ! " I was able to bear up under the blow, realizing that too serious a view should not be taken of fantail delinquencies !

Leaving fantails in the background, I felt very grateful to my son, who had, in buying me my London house, given me the opportunity of meeting again so many of my friends and going to various concerts. On the other hand, the mountain of years now heaped on me prevents me somewhat from rushing hither and thither as I used to do in my search of sweet sounds. I therefore console myself with my piano. Sir Edward Elgar [1] and his charming wife (now, alas! taken from us) were very great friends of mine for many years and I am still fortunate in retaining his friendship. Can any of our contemporary English composers ever be compared with him! His " Gerontius," " Apostles," Concertos for Violin, his Variations, " Cockaigne," and many others of his wondrous compositions drive me wild with delight whenever I am fortunate enough to hear them. Great as he is, he is extraordinarily kind. When I told him that I felt it rather dull playing by myself, and how anxious I was to find someone possessed of a fiddle who might be persuaded to come to my house and do music with me en tête-à-tête, he said, " Oh yes, my dear, I will tell a friend of mine to go and do some music with you." " Thank you, Edward," I said, imagining that he would pick out an unknown instrumentalist from one of his orchestras who would condescend to come and play with me. Imagine, therefore, my surprise when Sir Edward wrote and informed me that W. H. Reed, so well known to music lovers for his delightful compositions, his beautiful playing on the violin and as Leader of the Symphony Orchestra, was the friend he was sending as partner to my ramblings

[1] Since I wrote these lines my dear friend has left the world.

on the piano! As a matter of fact, Edward Elgar and W. H. Reed are great friends, and although he acquiesced, I feel sure that he did not look forward with much joy to such a task. At any rate, one morning he appeared. A bit cold in his manner, I thought, as with a professional air he took his violin out of its case. "What would you like to play?" he asked sternly. "I don't know," I answered, tremblingly. . . . "Bach—Mozart—Beethoven—Schumann?" "We can try the Bach Sonata in D," he said, in a weary way. Then we began, and his superb rendering of it made me completely forget myself. And he was not one bit angry at the end, but actually suggested a Beethoven Sonata. I then became quite happy and wondered at it all. Maybe our dear Elgar, great friend to us both, may have been present in our minds and his aura, enwrapping us, had power to make Willie Reed more lenient and uplift my nervous renderings into higher and more musical understanding! Since that morning the great violinist and I have become good friends. He even condescended to play the " Kreutzer " Sonata with me for gramophone records! I have, since then, been composing a little epitaph for my tombstone. Instead of R.I.P. I mean to have " In the Year of Our Lord 1931 She, here below, recorded the ' Kreutzer ' Sonata with W. H. Reed for the Gramophone! "

I am now about to harp once more on the delight of making friends, at whatever age you may attain. Now listen to this. I was in my library, alone with my little dog, writing these reminiscences. The wireless was turned on; and suddenly I heard the Queen's Hall B.B.C. Orchestra playing Greig's Concerto, the pianist being simply superb. I stopped writing and listened to it, entranced. When it was over I was so carried away that I cried Brava! Brava!— thumped on the table, stamped on the floor, Vimmy, my small dog, barking vociferously and joining in the noise. My servants, sitting at supper downstairs, rushed up in a body, imagining the house to be on fire. The Enchantress was Katharine Goodson, quite unaware of the excitement she had provoked at 2, Albert Road.

There it was! Nothing for it! I had to write to her! I begged her to come and play to me one day for an hour alone and let me drink in her exquisite music. She actually came, and nothing I can say can give any idea of what I think of her genius on the piano. And with it all she is one of the most charmingly modest creatures I have ever met. Now what I should have missed had I not, there and then, after her marvellous performance, seized a pen and written and told her what delight her playing had given me. Many of my friends say to me, "How *can* you write to people when they have not been introduced to you?" But I say that those favoured beings are the property of the world at large, and why, when their work has seized hold of you, should you not write and tell them so and say " Please let me know you, for in so doing you would lift me nearer to the stars " ?   I have made one or two very dear friends by my brushing aside of the rules of convention.   I will now mention another wonderful artist who, with his charming wife, has become a great friend of my later years—Arthur Watts. I imagine that many subscribers to *Punch* will remember a delightful and, to me, pathetic, coloured drawing which appeared in the Christmas number some two years ago.   It was called " Homesickness " and portrays a small monkey, tricked out in a little red coat and cap, who has broken the chain that ties him to a barrel-organ owned by a villainous-looking ruffian, and is making his way across the road towards a cart filled with palms and tropical plants, pushed along by two other horrible-looking men, half hidden by the green branches.   A few rather stupid-looking men and women are looking on at the small animal's antics, the only sympathetic creature watching the scene being a white horse, who, with a kindly expression, is turning its head, evidently understanding the monkey in its attempt to reach freedom.   The picture made a profound impression on me.   I knew Arthur Watts' work and had admired it much, but this particular drawing aroused all sorts of sorrowful feelings in my heart.   No help for it—I must write to Arthur Watts !   We had not met—but never mind !   " Dear Mr. Watts," I wrote, " I do so

love your picture—I have often felt like the
monkey. And, if it does not cost hundreds,
might I have it for my very own ? " And then—
oh joy !—an answer came . . . " It does not
cost hundreds and here is the picture . . .! "
What pleasure it has given me ! I had it framed
and it goes with me everywhere (it is on my table
now as I write). Then I got to know Arthur
Watts and his delightful wife and child and we
meet frequently. And thus *another* lovely friendship has enriched my life.

As I come to the end of my life's happenings I
realize that one must choose one's friends amongst
those possessing tastes and idiosyncrasies resem-
bling one's own and not in the bosom of one's
family. For instance, the great *trait d'union*
between W. H. Hudson and myself was our love
of birds. What knowledge he imparted to me
on the subject ! Then Henry James, without the
least show of superiority, used to discuss literature
with me. And now, this wonderful new friend
of mine, Katharine Goodson, talks to me about
my beloved music.

Many dear friends do I possess even now, too
numerous to mention, who take pity on my old
age and pay me frequent visits. My pen will not
stay quiet until I write the name of my very dear
friend Sir William Rothenstein. He really ought
to have left the world long ago, worn out by all
the good he has accomplished in it ! All those I
have mentioned are great artists and I hug to myself

the conviction that throughout my life friends have proved the important thing in it.

But, mind you, whilst I wave off Family with a big F, I do not mean those who are most closely related to one. I should be ungrateful indeed were I not to state here the tender love and affection that have always existed between my three sons and myself: Vyner, now Rajah of Sarawak, Bertram, his younger brother, and Harry, who left the world a few years ago but whose dear spirit remains at my side every hour of the day. No mother has ever been blessed with nobler or kinder sons than they. And then my grandchildren are also a source of constant happiness to me. To begin with, Vyner's three daughters, Leonora, Elizabeth and Valerie, Leonora being married to Lord Inchcape. Bertram's children: Jean, who married Tom Halsey; Elizabeth, who is Terence Maunsell's wife; Anne, as yet unmarried, and Peter. Lastly, James, my dear son Harry's boy.

Day in, day out, they come and look after Grandmama. They laugh at her jokes and are kind and lenient to her foibles and treat her as though she were as young as themselves. These silly children pretend I am not really old, that I do not look my age! If that is so it is owing to their love and the dear friendship that exists between us.

Together with these consolations there is another pleasure that lies behind old age: for the older we become the more we admire and love Nature.

We find God Almighty, that Friend of Friends, present in all things: in clouds and mists and red-rose sunsets; in moonlit nights and stars. Then we remember Venus, the Star of Love, where, maybe, we will meet our friends again in Paradise.

POSTSCRIPT

SINCE writing the last words of *Good Morning and Good Night*, my beloved friend, Maggie Ponsonby, has left the world. The memory of her generous nature, her keen sense of fun, her never-failing loyalty, helpfulness and kindness must remain for ever in the hearts of those who loved her.

APPENDIX

SARAWAK

Population estimated, 1871 . . . 200,000
"   "   1932 . . . 470,000

To-day there are :—Hospitals at Kuching, Sadong, Betong, Saratok, Simanggang, Sibu, Mukah, Bintulu, Miri, Baram, Limbang and Lawas. Dispensaries at Bau, Bukit Stubon, Sarikei and Miri. Pauper Camp and Leper Hospital some miles out of Kuching.

Schools. Government Vernacular and Chinese Schools all over the country. The S.P.G. and R.C. have large schools in Kuching and others over various parts of the country.

Public Buildings in Kuching are :

> Government Offices,
> Post Office,
> Museum,
> Library,
> Fire Station,
> New Police Barracks,
> Vegetable Market,
> Fish Market,
> Cinema,
> Chartered Bank of India, etc.,
> Ice Plant.

Water is supplied from Matong, eight miles away, and the town is lighted by electricity. There are excellent water supplies in all the principal towns.

WIRELESS STATIONS: Kuching Town, Kuching
Sub-Station, Lundu, Simanggang, Saratok,
Sibu, Binatang, Kapit, Mukah, Matu, Bintulu,
Belangian, Tatau, Miri, Baram, Limbang,
Lawas, Rejang, Kanowit.

INDEX